CoreWellness
A Physician Wellness Program

Jeffrey Levy, MD and Louis Neipris, MD

CaseNetwork Publishing
2019

CoreWellness: A Physician Wellness Program

This book was published by CaseNetwork Publishing.

Copyright © 2019 by Jeffrey Levy, MD and Louis Neipris, MD. All rights reserved. No part of this book may be reproduced or transmitted in any form or by any means, electronic or mechanical, including photocopying, recording, or by any information storage or retrieval system, without written permission from the publisher. For information address CaseNetwork Publishing at info@casenetwork.com.

Printed in the United States of America.

Edited by Catherine A. Johnson.
Cover design by Jeffrey Levy, MD.

www.casenetwork.com

DEDICATION

I dedicate this book to my family, who has had the courage to overcome serious adversities and approach them as opportunities for growth.

- Jeffrey Levy, MD

CONTENTS

INTRODUCTION 1

CHAPTER 1: BURNOUT 11

CHAPTER 2: WELLNESS 19

CHAPTER 3: RESILIENCE 25

CHAPTER 4: INTRODUCTION TO RESILIENCE EXERCISES 37

CHAPTER 5: MIND PULSE EXERCISE 43

CHAPTER 6: EMOTIONAL TEMPERATURE EXERCISE 51

CHAPTER 7: THOUGHT X-RAY AND –OMETER EXERCISES 61

CHAPTER 8: POSITIVE EVIDENCE POINTS EXERCISE 77

CHAPTER 9: THOUGHT-BALLOON EXERCISE 91

CHAPTER 10: NUCLEUS BELIEFS EXERCISE 95

CHAPTER 11: GAUSSIAN THOUGHT-DISTRIBUTION EXERCISE 101

CHAPTER 12: NARRATIVE MEDICINE EXERCISE 111

CHAPTER 13: PERSONAL MISSION STATEMENT EXERCISE 123

CHAPTER 14: CRASH CART RESILIENCE EXERCISE 131

CHAPTER 15: MANAGING CONFLICTS EXERCISE 137

CHAPTER 16: SELF-ASSESSMENT TOOLS 143

CHAPTER 17: WELLNESS PROGRAM EXAMPLES 149

CHAPTER 18: THE RESIDENT'S ROLE IN CREATING A CULTURE OF WELLNESS 161

CHAPTER 19: CREATING AN EFFECTIVE WELLNESS INITIATIVE FOR YOUR DEPARTMENT 169

CHAPTER 20: QUIZ 193

REFERENCES 207

OTHER USEFUL RESOURCES 217

INDEX 221

ABOUT THE AUTHORS 223

ABOUT CASENETWORK 225

INTRODUCTION

The most important patient we have to take care of is the one in the mirror.

Robert Wah, MD
former President of the American Medical Association

Thriving as a Physician

CoreWellness: A Physician Wellness Program provides you with knowledge and practical skills to manage stress and adversities typical of medical school and post-graduate training. You will learn about burnout syndrome (BOS), improve resilience, and achieve self-awareness through proactive wellness and self-care measures. This comprehensive program is the first of its kind, designed to help you cope with the unique demands of the healthcare profession and to better understand the impact stressors have on your cognitive, emotional, and physical well-being. This book provides information to help you not only survive your training, but to actually thrive and flourish.

Well-known psychologist and father of positive psychology, Dr. Martin Seligman, defined flourishing as the general ability to find fulfillment in life through positive emotion, accomplishing meaningful and worthwhile tasks, and deeply connecting with others to form meaningful relationships. Wellness can also be more broadly categorized, as was done by the U.S. Department of Health and Human Services Substance Abuse and Mental Health Services Administration,[1] to include eight dimensions:

1. **Emotional**: coping effectively with life and creating satisfying relationships.
2. **Environmental**: good health by occupying pleasant, stimulating environments that support well-being.
3. **Financial**: satisfaction with current and future financial situations.
4. **Intellectual**: recognizing creative abilities and finding ways to expand knowledge and skills.
5. **Occupational**: personal satisfaction and enrichment from one's work.
6. **Physical**: recognizing the need for physical activity, healthy foods, and sleep.
7. **Social**: developing a sense of connection, belonging, and a support system.
8. **Spiritual**: expanding a sense of purpose and meaning in life.

By reading this book and diligently completing the skill-building exercises, these wellness characteristics will become realistic and attainable and you will gain a solid understanding of BOS. More importantly, you will master the skills to nurture and maintain wellness during training and throughout your medical career. Although you can do these exercises alone, it is even more effective to do them within a trusted group. This will foster comradery, sharing, and expose you to different perspectives. The exercises are also intended to be complementary to any existing wellness offerings within your department or institution.

A Nature Analogy

We liken the growth you will experience in this program to growth in nature. Like a sapling tree growing during its first season, you may find yourself swaying in the wind during your early training. Trust that as you forge ahead, you will grow with experience. You will not be knocked down.

The delicate sapling thickens from season to season. Its stem becomes a strong, woody trunk whose concentric rings hold the secret of growing conditions each year. Eventually, the tree joins the canopy, a delicate ecosystem high above the forest. You, too, will be strong and seasoned, reach your long-term goal sooner than you think, and join the community of doctors practicing in your chosen specialty.

The young tree's life is not without setbacks. Dry seasons, early frosts, and overcrowding of the forest are among the stressors of an arboreal reality. To reach the sun-drenched canopy, whether through phototropism or other innate processes, the tree survives and flourishes by acting on its innate behavior. In some rudimentary way, the tree might even "learn" from year to year; before developing its tough first layer of protective bark, the sapling has responded adaptively to its environment. Likewise, competing the program outlined in this book will help you to adapt, grow, and thrive in the milieu of rigorous study and hospital-based training.

Wellness for Residents and Medical Students

Wellness does not always come naturally. Residents and medical students are certainly not plants or trees, but complex human beings. To many people, especially those stressed by illness, famine, war, or other factors beyond one's control, well-being—especially the wellness domain called "resilience"—is a learned set of skills.

The World Health Organization (WHO) recognizes that well-being encompasses more than physical health or the absence of infirmity. Moreover, the WHO considers emotional health as equally important.[2] It therefore follows that wellness—and even thriving—are possible for anyone willing to learn about their emotions and how they respond to stressors, and then try out new ways of thinking and living. How else could someone with diabetes or some other chronic illness self-manage their condition, go on with their life, and even thrive? The key to universal thriving is the ability to rise above circumstances by drawing on inner strengths and to learn emotional coping—this is the gateway to healthy behavior change.[2]

Of course residents and medical students are not the general population. A unique and useful definition of wellness applies to post-graduate trainees and medical students, as it would for any subpopulation (whether it be firefighters, marines, or refugees). It probably comes as no surprise that adequate sleep, a nutritious diet and exercise, and social connectedness with community, family and friends are important to residents and medical students. Why, then, are these obvious self-care practices set aside, postponed, or frankly ignored during the long road through medical school and hospital-based training?

Deficits in these basic human needs become risks for burnout, an imbalance between work demands and coping ability, which generally continues to worsen throughout medical school and affects between 50-75% of residents.[3,4] The high prevalence of burnout among post-graduate trainees is, in part, due to deficits in two other dimensions of well-being that are especially challenging to nurture[5]:

- **Autonomy**: having a say in shaping one's learning environment so that it supports well-being as much as clinical education, providing supervision commensurate with a graduated level of independence and responsibility.
- **Competence**: a sense of self-efficacy that increases through training as one accumulates positive experiences of successful patient care resulting from a resident's knowledge and skills.

These wellness dimensions, as well as physical and emotional health considerations, are important to address as individuals. The learning environment/training program must also take an active role in fostering a community of well-being where seeking help is not discouraged, but rather encouraged. In the tough-it-out, self-sacrificing realm of post-graduate training, residents may ignore one or more wellness dimensions. The results could be BOS, depression, or even suicide. Remember that the converse is true: nurturing wellness helps residents grow and thrive, even during the longest of on-call nights and in the most stressful of situations.

Recognizing Burnout

The Accreditation Council for Graduate Medical Education (ACGME) and the Association of American Medical Colleges expect residents and medical students to recognize signs of burnout to help minimize related patient care errors and any lapses in professionalism. Do you recognize BOS in others? If so, what do you do about it when you see it? More importantly, would you recognize BOS in yourself? Do you have BOS now, or is it possible you will get it sometime in the future, possibly during your training or after?

You may know some colleagues who appear especially irritable and feel down, anxious, or even hopeless about their future. Signs of BOS may be hard to recognize and they can be easily mistaken for many other mental health problems or physical illnesses. Also, one bad day does not a diagnosis of burnout make; we all have tough days.[6]

Let's look at a few examples of residents and medical students who have BOS or who are at risk for burnout. Although these cases are not based on real people, they are inspired by trainees who struggle with the same kinds of stressors you may encounter: social isolation, work-life balance, coping with loss, and grief. They all have in common some deficit or lack of attention to a wellness dimension. These examples are by no means intended to be representative of all residents and medical students, but they are evocative of common issues trainees struggle with and can overcome. See if you identify with any of them.

Mental Health Issues

John, a first-year resident, is starting to feel increasingly irritable, even during days when he is rested. His rotations, lectures, and rounds all seem to be going well, but it is becoming more difficult than he expected to maintain a positive outlook, especially when much of his day is spent entering notes and orders on time, only to have to clarify them later. He describes how constant pages distract him from the task of patient care, while days and on-call nights seem to chip away at his hope for a fulfilling career in medicine. He is starting to have second thoughts about becoming a physician. These doubts make him feel increasingly isolated, anxious, and somewhat ashamed as he finds it harder to thrive among his hard-working, focused, and dedicated colleagues.

Grappling With Grief

Miya, a third-year medical student, appears tired and disheveled. When asked a question by a senior resident, she appears preoccupied and does not make eye contact. She grimaces and frowns when hearing about an incoming patient. The senior resident is worried that Miya has not recovered from the death of a patient last week, one that she had admitted who had end-stage pancreatic cancer. This was the first death Miya experienced during her clinical rotations, and she seems to be taking it very hard. The next day she fails to show up for morning rounds, which is very concerning.

Striving for Work-Life Balance

Nicole, a third-year resident, had just returned home after an overnight call when she sees a note her husband left on the refrigerator. Without reading the message, she knows what he wrote: again, she missed an important event in her three-year-old daughter's life. Again, despite her best efforts to leave work on time, her husband played father and mother. "The birthday party…" Nicole sighs to herself as she hangs up her jacket. She walks into the kitchen, feeling hunger pangs, knowing what the rest of the note would say: "No worries, the freezer is freshly stocked with your favorite frozen dinners. Take your pick!" The remaining sentences confirm what she fears. In matter-of-fact, non-blaming, neutral language, her spouse conveyed the scheduling reality, explaining that he waited for her but had to leave with their daughter so she could arrive on time to her best friend's birthday party.

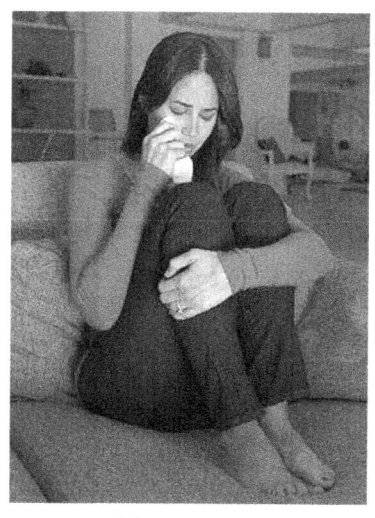

Overcome With Anxiety

Jamar is a second-year medical student. He is extremely sleep deprived, but not because of any clinical responsibilities. He hasn't been able to sleep because his USMLE is in two weeks and he is panicking that he is going to fail. All of his classmates have been studying the same amount or less than he has, but they seem so much more confident. Jamar thinks there must be something wrong with him. Every time he puts his head on the pillow to try to sleep, all of his negative thoughts start racing through his head and he can't shut them off.

What to Expect From This Book

CoreWellness: A Physician Wellness Program will help you build new knowledge and learn skills that will improve your wellness and resilience. Each chapter is briefly described below.

Chapter 1: Burnout – The definition of burnout is provided, as well as its etiology, prevalence, and consequences. The diagnosis of burnout is also described.

Chapter 2: Wellness – Factors associated with wellness in residency and medical school and a "culture of wellness" are described. Wellness measurements and interventions are also provided.

Chapter 3: Resilience – The concept of resilience and its relationship to cognitive behavioral therapy is described. Resilience measurement tools are provided.

Chapter 4: Introduction to Resilience Exercises – This chapter describes how skill-building training works and how you can get the most out of the resilience exercises described in this book. You will learn about the concepts of You-Guru and You-Dini.

Chapter 5: Mind Pulse Exercise – This exercise is an introduction to the way you think and will reveal thinking patterns that will be useful in subsequent exercises.

Chapter 6: Emotional Temperature Exercise – This exercise helps increase self-awareness of how adversities affect emotions. It will help you discover, analyze, and enhance self-awareness regarding events or stressors that trigger strong emotions in you.

Chapter 7: Thought X-Ray and -Ometer Exercises – These self-discovery exercises will help you to take a deeper look into your thinking, especially at overly intense or counterproductive emotional/behavioral responses generated by cognitive distortions.

Chapter 8: Positive Evidence Points Exercise – This exercise will help you focus on techniques to build self-esteem through positive self-affirming statements and by documenting benchmark achievements and positive feedback from colleagues, faculty, and mentors.

Chapter 9: Thought-Balloon Exercise – This is a thought exercise for challenging unhelpful beliefs using breathwork and visualization.

Chapter 10: Nucleus Beliefs Exercise – This exercise helps you get past the surface beliefs and detect your core beliefs – those deep-rooted beliefs of how you view yourself, others, the future, and the world.

Chapter 11: Gaussian Thought-Distribution Exercise – This exercise will help you improve the accuracy of your thinking and put things in perspective by using a probability distribution to determine the likelihood that an event will actually occur.

Chapter 12: Narrative Medicine Exercise – This exercise teaches the concept of narrative medicine and describes three simple steps to nurture empathy and compassion, both individually and in groups.

Chapter 13: Personal Mission Statement Exercise – In this exercise you will learn to craft a mission statement, describing your overall purpose for going into medicine as well as the meaning of day-to-day life as a physician-in-training.

Chapter 14: Crash Cart Resilience Exercise – This chapter teaches you how to relax using breathwork and visualization when confronted with stressors.

Chapter 15: Managing Conflicts Exercise – This exercise teaches you how to diffuse anger as a first step toward conflict resolution. Once tempers are calm, the work of negotiation and problem solving can begin.

Chapter 16: Self-Assessment Tools – 26 self-assessment tools and questionnaires are provided in this chapter, allowing you to explore your perceptions and views of yourself, others, and your future on a regular basis.

Chapter 17: Wellness Program Examples – This chapter describes several wellness models that have been implemented in residency programs, have been published, have demonstrated efficacy, and have strong approval-ratings among participants.

Chapter 18: The Resident's Role in Creating a Culture of Wellness – This chapter describes how residents can lead the effort to build and maintain a culture of wellness within their training programs.

Chapter 19: Creating an Effective Wellness Initiative for Your Department – This chapter describes a step-by-step approach to design, launch, and maintain a wellness initiative.

Chapter 20: Quiz – A series of questions will test your knowledge and determine your grasp of materials presented in this book.

It is important to note that this program is not a substitute for professional individual or group therapy for mental health issues, especially for individuals with depression or suicide ideation. The outcome of this program will be different for each individual, team, department, and institution. The program will be affected by the amount of time and effort individuals devote to the resilience exercises, the ability to have group interactions within a trusting and safe environment, and the desire and effort to foster a culture of wellness at the institutional level.

CHAPTER 1
BURNOUT

The land of burnout is not a place I ever want to go back to.

Arianna Huffington, Author

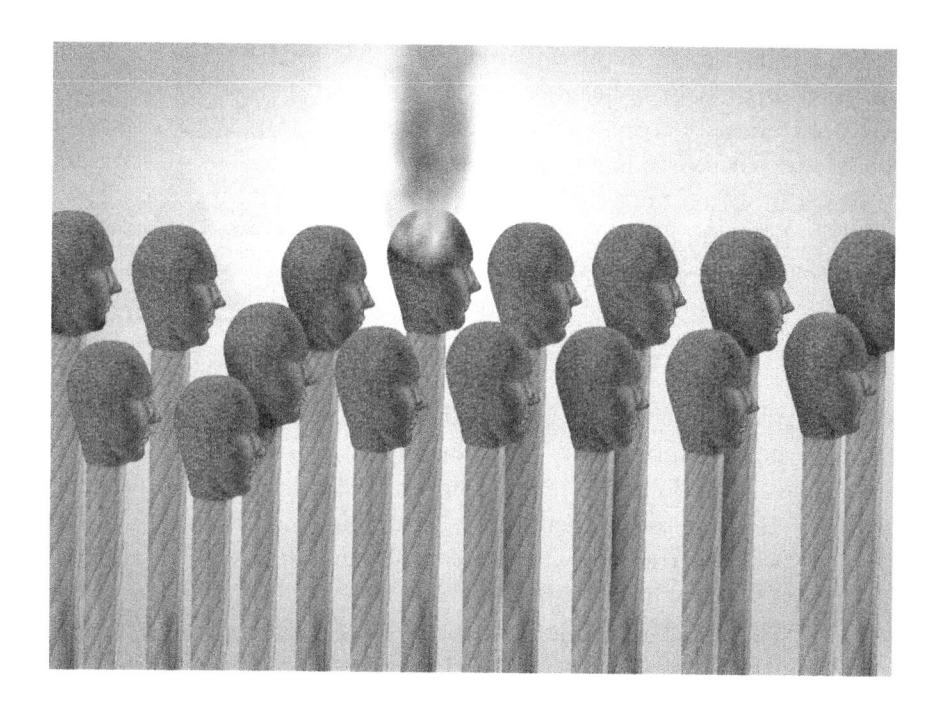

Introduction to Burnout

During any conference or lecture, take a moment to notice your peers sitting around you. Maybe the person on your left is on the same rotation with you. Perhaps the person in front of you just signed out her patients to you, is post-call, and is nodding off a little. You know their names and you probably even grumble and complain with them now and again. That's just part of training. Or is it?

Did you know that, according to national surveys, as many as three out of four of your colleagues may be suffering from burnout syndrome (BOS)?[4] Burnout and depression often coexist during training, but trainees often do not seek help—out of denial, shame, concern over confidentiality, or for other reasons.

Many residency programs and medical schools have resources in place to help trainees with burnout and depression, or for those who are in crisis. Getting help is important, both for the healthcare provider and for the patients they treat. Medical errors are more likely to occur in trainees who have BOS, and such errors can lead physicians to carry a heavy burden of self-blame and even consider suicide. Up to 12% of doctors with BOS express thoughts of suicide, and the rate of completed suicide in medical trainees is double that of the general population.[4] That is why recognizing BOS can help not only to sustain a career, but to literally save lives.

Definition

Burnout syndrome is a prolonged, psychological response to job-related, interpersonal stressors. It is especially common among healthcare professionals at all career stages, including residents and medical students. BOS occurs when occupational demands exceed

one's ability to cope, and is characterized by three measurable domains[7]:
1. **Emotional Exhaustion**: feelings of emotional and physical depletion.
2. **Depersonalization:** a sense of indifference, detachment, or negative, cynical feelings toward patients and/or co-workers.
3. **Lack of Personal Efficacy:** a decreased sense of personal accomplishment.

Etiology

Occupational stressors leading to BOS accumulate during the preclinical training years, finally reaching a critical point during the later years of medical school or shortly after starting residency. Without improved coping ability during the first months of internship, as the workday becomes longer and patient responsibility increases, those more susceptible to BOS struggle to put present-day challenges in perspective. They may lose sight of the greater goal of graduating residency and going into practice. These are the residents who begin to manifest signs and symptoms of burnout, if they have not already done so prior to graduating from medical school.

The extent to which personality traits and work-related stressors contribute to BOS is still the subject of debate. Research has uncovered a statistically significant correlation with two of the three burnout domains—emotional exhaustion and depersonalization—and several broad personality types, including[8]:
- **Neuroticism**: a high level of negative emotions and reactivity to stressful situations.
- **Alexithymia**: reduced ability to recognize or describe one's feelings.

BOS is also more likely in people who are overwhelmed or emotionally burdened by work-related stressors such as[7]:
- work overload, contributing to emotional depletion

- lack of control over burdensome details or processes, eroding a sense of professional accomplishment
- insufficient reward or recognition for day-to-day accomplishments, leading to low personal achievement

Other factors related to BOS include[3]:
- feelings of isolation
- grief or self-blame over poor patient outcome
- harassment on the job

ETIOLOGY: Harassment, Work overload, Self-blame, Lack of control, Feelings of isolation, Insufficient recognition

Beware the Tough-It-Out Attitude

A subtler, unspoken factor leading to BOS is the training ethos that healthcare providers must do all for their patients, even at the expense of meeting their own personal needs. In such a learning culture, residents and medical students take on a suffering-is-noble attitude while struggling in silence. However, the healer-superhero persona is a myth. Doctors—whether residents, medical students, or established practitioners—are also human beings who are vulnerable, not invincible.

There is a stigma associated with seeking help. Residency programs and medical schools are increasingly proactive, teaching trainees to recognize signs of burnout and depression. A training milieu that does not actively raise this self-awareness and de-stigmatize mental illness, while making residents and medical students feel safe to pursue confidential services, is an environment more conducive to BOS.[9]

Prevalence

Multiple studies indicate that burnout rates steadily increase during medical school and range from about 40% to over 70% among residents across several specialties. There is a notable increase in BOS during the first few months of residency according to the results of anonymous, cross-training surveys. With the rise in burnout, there is a corresponding increased risk of depression: at 15% during medical school to over 30% during post-graduate training.[3,10]

Burnout prevalence continues to remain high among practitioners, exceeding 60% in emergency medicine, between 50%-60% of physicians in general internal medicine, neurology, and family medicine, and approximately 50% in otolaryngology, orthopedic surgery, anesthesia, and obstetrics and gynecology.[3,11]

Consequences of Burnout

Burnout may seem to be a purely personal issue, but in medicine that is not the case. The enormous burden that residents and medical students on rotation undertake to maintain patient quality-of-care could result in BOS with detrimental effects on the trainees' personal lives and professional development. However, burnout also leads to negative ramifications for patients.[3]

Professional Consequences
- gaps in professionalism, including callous attitudes or overt hostility toward patients and co-workers
- lack of career satisfaction
- early retirement or leaving the profession

Personal Consequences
- strained relationships, marital separation, or divorce
- depression and anxiety
- suicidal ideation/completed suicides

Patient Consequences
- increased medical errors
- less patient satisfaction with quality of care

Making a Diagnosis of Burnout Syndrome

BOS occurs gradually and insidiously anywhere along the health career continuum, from medical school to residency or even during professional practice. Among other validated instruments, a 22-item self-reported questionnaire called the Maslach Burnout Inventory (MBI) is often used to diagnose BOS based on scoring the frequency of three domains of burnout.[7] The three domains are emotional exhaustion, depersonalization, and reduced personal accomplishments.

Emotional Exhaustion
Depersonalization
Reduced Personal Accomplishments

Emotional Exhaustion

Also referred to as vital exhaustion, this is a loss of energy and feeling depleted or fatigued. It may be experienced first in response to a new working environment or in a current occupational setting when change brings about new demands exceeding one's coping ability.

Depersonalization

Also called cynicism, depersonalization is a negative detachment from work, in which physicians act impersonally with patients and staff. It can also deteriorate to unprofessional behavior, for example directing cynical remarks at patients, coworkers, or both.

Lack of Personal Efficacy

Also known as inefficacy, this refers to an excessive, unfounded sense of incompetence or failure, a self-image that is not reflective of what peers may perceive as a high level of achievement and job proficiency.

Burnout and Related Diagnoses

There is overlap between signs and symptoms of BOS and psychiatric and medical diagnoses. The diagnostic "grey zone" is especially apparent between BOS and depression, anxiety, and sleep disorders.

Psychological and Emotional Features
- anxiety
- anhedonia
- hopelessness
- anger and frustration

Physical Signs and Symptoms
- fatigue
- headaches
- muscle tension
- gastrointestinal problems
- difficulty falling or staying asleep

Experts generally agree that an *occupational context* is consistently associated with burnout, while multiple settings (as well as variable extrinsic and intrinsic factors outside the workplace) increase the risk of depressive disorders. However, others maintain that BOS is insufficiently differentiated from depression and recommend against viewing the two as separate illnesses. A study of more than five thousand participants demonstrated that 90% of individuals fit the criteria for both BOS and depression.[12]

ACGME Mandate

In 2003, in the face of increasing evidence that sleep deprivation and exhaustion compromise cognitive abilities, the Accreditation Council for Graduate Medical Education (ACGME) mandated a reduction in the maximum number of consecutive duty hours for all residents. However, work hour restriction, while facilitating schedule flexibility, did not improve patient outcomes and had little impact on trainee quality-of-life. Moreover, these changes were insufficient to reduce the rate of BOS.[3] A more comprehensive approach to reform the post graduate training environment was needed, leading to the ACGME's requirement the that all residency programs create a learning and working environment that fosters self-care, a skill that must be "learned and nurtured" as part of residency training.[13]

Wellness interventions are as varied as the needs of the trainee populations where these initiatives are implemented. The *CoreWellness* curriculum was therefore developed to provide some standardization for wellness interventions, and serves as a supplement to existing departmental and institutional wellness initiatives.

CHAPTER 2
WELLNESS

The secret of health for both mind and body is not to mourn for the past, not to worry about the future, or not to anticipate troubles, but to live in the present moment wisely and earnestly.

Buddha

Introduction to Well-Being

The general public is more likely to associate "house officer" with the self-sacrificing good doctor, working hard in the regimented, rigorous realm of hospital-based training than with a resident or medical student who practices good self-care. However, if your program is among the growing number that values trainee/student well-being, "house officer" or "resident" may evoke not only a sense of duty toward patients, but also fun and relaxation with colleagues, family, and friends. Softball games, volleyball on the beach, movie night, working out at a nearby gym where your program subsidizes your membership, perhaps even an on-call room refrigerator stocked with nutritious foods—these aspects are increasingly integral to the concept of a resident or medical student striving for work-life balance as well as professional excellence. Even if not particulars of your program's self-care experience, these are real and vital components of other residencies and medical schools that have taken steps to nurture a culture of wellness.

What is a Culture of Wellness?

A residency program or medical school is considered to have a culture of wellness if it supports a healthy workforce (which includes residents, medical students, and faculty) who value self-care as a means of maintaining high-quality patient care. In a culture of wellness, the commitment toward a physically and emotionally healthy workforce exists on two levels[14]:

- Organizational leadership promotes specific wellness interventions with tools and resources; and
- At the same time, residents

and medical students feel safe to engage administration in ongoing dialogue toward sustainable and dynamic efforts that meet trainees' changing needs.

The Well-Being House

Think of wellness as a house with several rooms, called *domains*, such as physical, emotional, and spiritual health, among others. It is not only possible to live in a well-being house, but it is now an ACGME mandate for residency programs to develop wellness initiatives. Remember that self-care is not selfish or self-indulgent, but instead conducive to better patient outcomes.[15] You have a right to your wellness home. Taking care of yourself helps you to become a better, more capable doctor.

You, too, can help sustain and evolve a culture of wellness in your medical school or training program. The first step is to learn what wellness means to you and how your own definition of well-being is unique compared to those outside of medicine. Practicing well-being is also easier if you understand your program's vision for a culture of wellness.

Definition

Ask five people to define "wellness" or "well-being" and you would likely receive five different descriptions. Most would agree that health is an important component, but they would not necessarily define it as the absence of disease. For example, think of patients with a terminal illness who clearly express a positive outlook, carry a sense of dignity, and appear to be at peace with themselves and the world around them. Accordingly, the World Health Organization recognizes a wider scope of wellness and describes it as an "optimal state of physical, mental/emotional and social well-being, and not merely the absence of disease."[2]

A large review examining over one hundred self-reported well-being measures widens the definition further to include the following domains[16]:

- **Spiritual**: a sense of connectedness to something greater than oneself; a sense that life has meaning.
- **Activities and Functioning**: deriving happiness when undertaking the tasks of daily life; how we fill our time.
- **Social Connectedness**: deep, enduring relationships; having social support.

As previously mentioned, the U.S. Department of Health and Human Services provided several other dimensions to the definition of wellness[1]:

- **Environmental**: good health by occupying pleasant, stimulating environments that support well-being.
- **Financial**: satisfaction with current and future financial situations.
- **Intellectual**: recognizing creative abilities and finding ways to expand knowledge and skills.
- **Occupational**: personal satisfaction and enrichment from one's work.

Factors Associated With Wellness During Medical Training

The residency and medical school experience concerns itself with wellness dimensions common to non-health professionals. However, based on extensive surveys of trainees, healthcare education with its unique stressors widens the wellness scope. A systematic review concluded that trainees are likely to associate wellness with the following attributes[5]:

- **Autonomy**: the perception that one has an appropriate level of responsibility in a learning environment that fosters mutual respect and teamwork, and positive feedback from mentors and colleagues.
- **Competence**: trainees experience how their clinical management results in positive clinical outcomes.

- **Social Support**: both within the program and from family and friends.
- **Physical Well-Being**: adequate exercise, sleep, and healthy eating.[5]
- **Emotional Health**: stress-reduction methods that teach a relaxation response founded on breathwork and movement, including yoga and tai chi.[3]

Familiarize yourself with your program's vision of wellness. You can then determine whether self-care interventions adequately address your needs and the needs of your peers.

Well-Being Measurements

How does one measure well-being? If the definition of well-being is so different among people and populations, how can such measurements be valid? Research in resident and medical student wellness seeks to answer both of these questions. In the meantime, several questionnaires, scales, and surveys can be used, each with its own set of strengths and weaknesses. Below are a few examples of well-being assessments used by residency programs and medical schools.

WHO-5

The WHO-5 is a shortened version of the WHO-10. Its five questions are designed to ascertain subjective measures of well-being. The maximum score is 25; a score below 13 is suggestive of poor mental well-being and an indication for further analysis.[17] Because the tool does not assess quality of life specific to the resident and medical student experience, the WHO-5 is best used in concert with other wellness assessments.

Satisfaction With Life Scale

The Satisfaction with Life Scale (SLS) presents five statements designed to assess overall fulfillment in life. A score between 20-24 is considered average. A score between 31-35 is very high (highly satisfied) and one between 5-9 is very low (extremely dissatisfied). A low score may correlate with depression or suicidal ideation.[5,18]

Postgraduate Hospital Education Environment Measure

Originally designed for the intensive care setting, the Postgraduate Hospital Education Environment Measure (PHEEM) is a cross-specialty tool for assessing a learner's attitudes toward the training environment. The subject's responses to 40 statements are designed to evaluate quality of education and well-being dimensions: autonomy, teaching, and social support. A score of greater than or less than 50 in each of the domains indicates overall satisfaction or dissatisfaction, respectively.[19]

Maslach Burnout Inventory and Patient Health Questionnaire

Strategies aimed at reducing the risk of burnout, depression or suicide may utilize the Maslach Burnout Inventory (MBI) and Patient Health Questionnaire-9 (PHQ-9). These instruments assess a wellness intervention's effect on BOS and the risk of major depression or suicidality.

For more information about how to access these well-being assessment tools, refer to Chapter 16, "Self-Assessment Tools."

CHAPTER 3
RESILIENCE

Our greatest glory is not in never falling,
but in rising every time we fall.

Confucius

Introduction to Resilience

Have you ever experienced an apparently quiet on-call night when suddenly the pings and pager beeps started to barrage you the moment you set your head down to rest? You got up, replaced an IV line that a patient pulled out, consoled family members, placed an NG tube, put out a few other fires, wrote orders, and hustled to complete your notes until morning rounds. What kept you moving, your spirits up, and your focus laser-sharp with an ability to multi-task—and maybe even laugh a little during that night? The answer is *resilience*.

Adapting well to adverse conditions, such as a challenging night on the wards, is only part of what resilience is about. How did you feel in the morning when, as you joined up with your team, they began to ask you to present the patients you admitted hours before? You may have felt tired but proud, having bounced back after some really uncertain moments. That ability to bounce back is also an important part of resilience, and it requires a deeper understanding of what it means to be resilient during medical training.

Definition

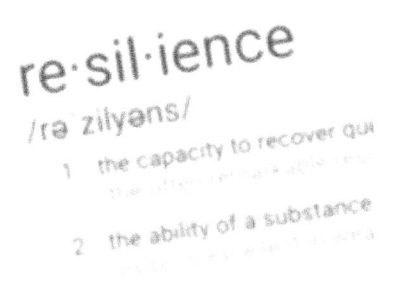

A simplified definition of resilience is the ability to recover in the face of adversity. At one time, a resilient individual was considered a hardy person, someone who remains strong, tolerant, and capable of holding up under pressure. Further research uncovers good news for the resident or medical student navigating the stressors of training: *everyone is capable of resilience*. Personality traits are just one of several attributes that are conducive to resilience.[20] Much of what builds resilience is a willingness to change, a process that begins with self-exploration.

Resilience training is therefore integral to wellness programs, helping residents and medical students learn their own coping styles and empowering them to recover from the stressors of training. Resilience skills improve with experience, enabling you not only to recover from small, irksome, day-to-day and night-after-night challenges, but also teaching you how to withstand catastrophe.[20,21]

Let's return to the on-call night we thought about a moment ago. What if the night had been different? What if things had not gone so well? Like a lot of healthcare professionals, you may have had to struggle with loss, a sense of guilt, or self-blame following the death of a patient under your care. For many physicians, overcoming such an emotional challenge takes experience and practice, beginning with learning the "ABC's" of resilient thinking.

The Resilience-Cognitive Behavioral Therapy Connection

Cognitive behavioral therapy (CBT) is a successful, evidenced-based psychotherapy used to treat a range of conditions, from posttraumatic stress to depression and anxiety disorders. Techniques drawn from CBT have also been shown to build resilience in well populations, including residents and medical students who are at risk for burnout, suicidal ideation, and other mental health conditions. When applied to graduate and postgraduate education, resilience exercises founded on CBT principles enhance emotional self-awareness and mindfulness, thereby reducing the risk of burnout and depression while improving measures of resilience.[15,22]

CBT is founded on three assumptions[23]:
1. Thought content, or cognitive activity, affects how we feel and act.
2. Cognitive activity can be changed through supportive self-monitoring.
3. Positive changes in thinking patterns can bring about desired outcomes including improved mood and behavior.

Making the ABC Thought Connections

How do you begin to positively change your thinking patterns? First, you must understand the relationship of ABC thought connections that are best described in CBT research.

A = Adversity or Stressor
Example: Within two hours of sign-out, after your colleagues have gone home, your on-call night is turning out to be the busiest ever.

B = Belief
Example 1: "I cannot deal with this and I am not confident things will work out; there will be so many patients that I'll make mistakes. A patient will die and that will be the end of my medical career."

Example 2: "Yes, there are a lot of patients at once, but I can ask for help and I will do the best I can. I can learn new organizational skills to handle this challenge, because it is not unlike what I have done before. This on-call night will be one I will remember, and it's going to turn out just fine.

C = Consequences (Feelings or Behaviors)
The C resulting from the belief in example 1 could be high-stress and a disorganized approach to the on-call challenge. This distressful consequence is a result of a type of cognitive distortion known as *catastrophizing*. When catastrophizing, one assumes the worst, most catastrophic outcome possible rather than assuming the most likely (a more neutral or positive) outcome.

The C resulting from the belief in example 2 is more likely to lead to appropriate coping with the situation, an acceptable stress level, and creative use of support services for processing patient admissions. Note how the thought content invokes reason, fact, and problem solving, unlike the dysfunctional, stress-inducing thought-stream in the first example.

Now you can understand how the ABC model helps explain our reactions to adversity.

Discover and Reinvent the ABC's of Your Mind

Like a novice boxer—open and unprotected—you may find that your training environment is becoming a painful boxing match, leaving you vulnerable to daily jabs and punches. You might be wondering, "Where are all those powerful, distressful feelings—my personal knock-out hits—coming from?" Your opponent is not another boxer, but the B's in the ABC's of your mind. The missing B's are like hidden left-hooks and uppercuts: inaccurate and distorted beliefs, non-factual thoughts, hidden beliefs, and thoughts that leave you vulnerable to distressing feelings and unhelpful behaviors. Keep your eye on your opponent, the unfounded B's—this self-awareness will help you to hold your hands high while keeping elbows low as you build a new line of defense with truthful, resilience-building beliefs.

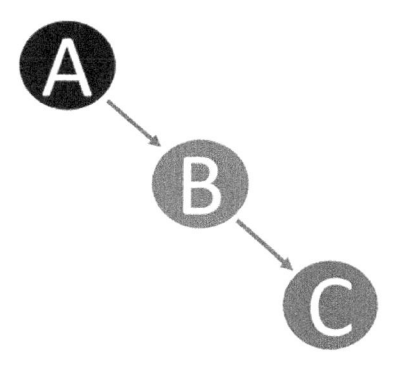

Your training needn't be round after round of painful boxing matches, but rather the challenging yet rewarding journey you want it to be. That journey begins with self-knowledge and creativity founded on the ABC cognitive-based model for uncovering old, dysfunctional beliefs and replacing them with well-founded and accurate assessments of the inevitable stressors and adversities you will encounter during medical training.[24]

Resilience and Neurophysiology

Teaching yourself to adopt new ways of thinking is not only possible based on cognitive behavioral methods, but also based on the neurophysiologic model of resilience. Research on posttraumatic stress, depression, and differences in resilience teach us that improved coping is related both to neuroplasticity and to developing new neuropathways and different, more adaptive and helpful ways of viewing stress.[25,26] The overall objective of resilience skill-building is to harness one's innate cognitive flexibility, leading to the ability to reappraise negative situations. Practicing the resilience exercises in this book will help you find meaning in stress, create more realistic and optimistic beliefs, and empower you not only to avoid distress and difficulties resulting from adversity, but also to learn, grow, and flourish personally and professionally.

A-to-C Connections Don't Occur Without B's

Most people think that there is a direct connection from the A's to the C's that we cannot control. Can an adversity happen that automatically leads to a consequence? The answer is no! There is always a B (thought/belief) in between the A and C that has a direct impact on the resulting consequence (the behavior or action). If your A's led directly to your C's, you would react to an adversity in the exact same way as everyone else. But that is not how it happens. Everyone reacts differently because everyone has unique thinking processes and patterns.

Let's think back to Miya, the third-year medical student who appeared tired and disheveled, and who grimaced and frowned when hearing about an incoming patient because she was having a difficult time dealing with the death of another patient. Even though the patient's death was not her fault, she was so distraught that the next day she failed to show up for morning rounds.

Probably almost all medical students and residents would be upset in a similar situation, but they would deal with it in different ways. Some would realize that the patient's death was not their fault, and would do everything they could to learn valuable lessons from the situation. Some would need to talk about it with their peers or faculty to process the loss. Some people would be upset for a day or two and then immerse themselves in the care of other patients. Others, like the student in this example, would be upset for months and not be able to continue with their day-to-day responsibilities as a healthcare provider. All of those possibilities are dependent on the individual's B's (their thoughts and beliefs).

Just like the boxing scenario from earlier, you can build your skills over time with deliberate practice and experience. You can learn to understand and control your B's to have a dramatic impact on your C's. We will explore how you can impact your thinking throughout the rest of this book.

Common Patterns of B-to-C Connections

As you get more in tune with your thinking, you might detect that some patterns emerge. You may begin to realize that you have some strong and consistent connections between your B's and C's.[27] For instance:

C: Feelings or Emotions	B: Beliefs or Thoughts
Anger	You perceive that your rights have been violated in some way.
Sadness or depression	You sense a loss of self-worth or that there is a real-world loss.
Guilt	You think you have violated someone else's rights.
Anxiety or fearfulness	You perceive some type of threat in the future.
Embarrassment	You are negatively comparing yourself to others.

Thinking More Accurately

Everyone can make some vital tweaks to their thinking in order to process reality differently and more constructively, accurately, and beneficially. All effective resilience-enhancing and coping methods begin with learning skills of self-awareness to find hidden B's (those dysfunctional beliefs based on established thought patterns that could derail you during an adversity). Let's look first at automatic thoughts and then explore core beliefs.

Automatic Thoughts

Automatic thoughts go unnoticed, but the strong emotions associated with them do not. The B's of automatic thinking need not drive distressful emotions or the C's (consequences) of a given stressor. For example, you may be about to park in a choice spot very close to the hospital entrance, when another driver pulls in first. You might immediately respond with tenseness and anger, or even swear.

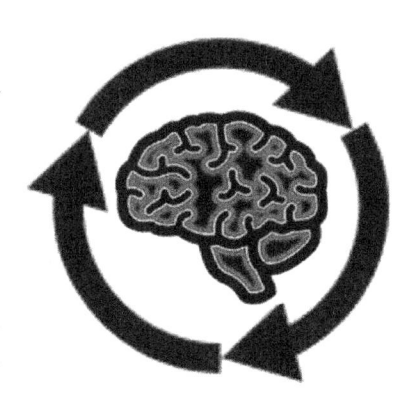

Where did such an extreme reaction come from? Most likely the driver that took your intended spot didn't even notice you trying to park. Perhaps the driver is a father whose child is having severe abdominal pain and needs to be rushed to the emergency room. Automatic thoughts eclipse such alternative possibilities in this situation and reflexively place blame: that the driver is selfish, thoughtless, careless, an unfair is a quick, imperceptible thought-stream that turns innocence into culpability, igniting your flash-fire of A-C connections and leading to anger without any consideration of the underlying, unfounded beliefs (the automatic B's).

Resilience training and exercises based on the ABC model will help you find the missing B's, those factual errors in thinking that underlie unhelpful emotions and behaviors.

Core Beliefs

Core beliefs are pervasive. Formed during childhood and molded through experience, core beliefs go under the radar of awareness much like automatic thoughts do. However, in contrast to automatic thoughts, core beliefs are not situation- or setting-specific. Rather, they tend to arise across life's domains: at home and at work, toward family and friends, and with regard to oneself. Some of these underlying beliefs, such as, "I am a good person," or "Being honest is very important to me," are very positive and lead to happiness and success. Other core beliefs can be maladaptive, such as believing "I am unlovable," or "I am incompetent." The latter are dysfunctional thinking patterns related to personal achievement, self-control, and dependency, among other areas.[28]

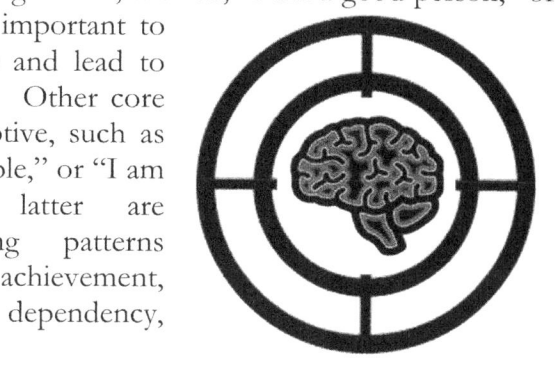

Certain deeply rooted core beliefs sometimes cause a B-C disconnect, meaning that the behavior seems inappropriate and the emotions seem out of proportion to the adversity. These types of core beliefs can make you more at risk for psychological problems, including depression and anxiety disorders.[29] Making ABC connections can help you to identify your core beliefs, but these hard-wired thought patterns may require more work and support to change. This will be further addressed in Chapter 10, "Nucleus Beliefs Exercise."

Characteristics of Resilience

The Resilience Domain: Your Well-Being Safe Place

Everyone can learn to become resilient during minor day-to-day adversities, but steering through life's major challenges takes more work and practice. Practicing resilience is not about retreating head-down into a storm cellar. It is about keeping your head up with an acute awareness of the situation along with your own thoughts and beliefs. It is about maintaining realistic optimism while undergoing emotional processing, learning self-compassion, and deriving support from others who have experienced similar losses. These are resilience strategies that can help you in the most difficult situations, and learning to use these strategies will reduce burnout.[15]

Not One-Size-Fits-All

There is no one-size-fits-all set of attributes that constitute resilience. Successful resilience skills may work for one person but not another. They are dependent on personality, context, and available resources. These are aspects of resilience accessible to anyone regardless of one's personality—tough and hardy or reactive and sensitive, anyone is capable of resilience.

Reflection
Emotional Regulation
Self-Efficacy

The following resilience traits are among several found to be helpful to residents and medical students, and are included in resilience training: reflection, emotional regulation, and self-efficacy.

- **Reflection**: The practice of sharing stressful experiences—through writing, art, story-telling, or by means of another form of expression—cultivates personal perspective in the face of challenge while building insight into human nature and compassion for patients.[30]
- **Emotional Regulation**: This refers to the capacity to cope with one's difficult feelings or first impulses toward negative thinking, in order to stay focused during stressful clinical or inter-professional encounters. Sometimes practiced through mindfulness techniques, these skills help you to regulate first impulses, facilitating a warm and caring demeanor with patients who are suffering. Resisting the initial impulse to respond with anger if you are confronted with unfair criticism, bullying, or harassment allows you to access assertive communication skills in the face of unprofessional behavior.[31]

- **Self-Efficacy**: The realization that physicians at all levels are capable of coping with grief following the loss of a patient, and that one can—and should—seek support when needed while maintaining realistic optimism in the practice of medicine.[20,22]

Measuring Resilience

Several validated measures of resilience are used as part of research into improving quality of life and wellness during medical school and in post-graduate training. These include the Connor-Davidson Resilience Scale and the Resilience Factor Inventory.

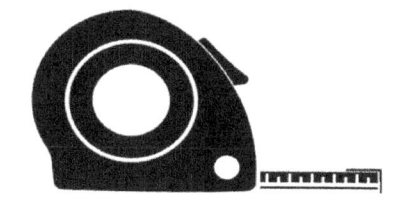

The Connor-Davidson Resilience Scale

The Connor-Davidson Resilience Scale (CD-25) is used to ascertain a person's strengths and vulnerabilities with respect to resilience attributes. Data derived from CD-25 questionnaires are often used to inform wellness programming and to determine the efficacy of resilience training. The similar Brief Resilience Scale (BRS) is a shorter, five-item questionnaire that assesses a person's ability to bounce back or recover following a stressful event.

Results of several multi-center studies across residency programs in different specialties prove that the CD-25 can be employed as a confidential assessment of five resilience attributes[32]:
1. personal competence
2. trust, tolerance, and strength in the face of stressors
3. acceptance of change and secure relationships
4. control over one's life
5. spiritual influences

The self-reported results are scored, with the sum of responses placing residents in three resilience categories:

Score	Resilience Category
<60	Low
70-79	Intermediate
80-100	High

One multi-center study revealed consistently lower baseline resilience scores among interns than those of the general population.[21] This result is important because resilience helps prevent burnout; low resilience levels are associated with more stress, depression, and BOS.

The Resilience Factor Inventory

The Resilience Factor Inventory, a 60-item questionnaire developed by Adaptiv Learning Systems, is another resilience assessment tool. It measures seven resilience factors that help determine an individual's ability to overcome life's hurdles. These seven factors are more fully described in the book *The Resilience Factor* by Karen Reivich, PhD and Andrew Shatte, PhD.[27] They include:

1. **Emotion Regulation**: the ability to control one's emotions in the face of adversity and to remain goal focused.
2. **Impulse Control**: the ability to control one's behavior in the face of adversity and remain goal focused.
3. **Causal Analysis**: the ability to accurately and comprehensively identify the causes of one's adversities and generate effective solutions.
4. **Self-Efficacy**: one's sense of mastery over adversity, challenges, and opportunities.
5. **Realistic Optimism**: a reality-based belief that the future is positive, due to one's causal analysis and self-efficacy skills.
6. **Empathy**: the ability to read the verbal and non-verbal cues of others to estimate their mental state and emotion.
7. **Reaching Out**: the ability to deepen relationships with others and to take on new challenges and opportunities.

For more information about how to access these and other resilience assessment tools, go to Chapter 16, "Self-Assessment Tools."

CHAPTER 4
INTRODUCTION TO
RESILIENCE EXERCISES

With the new day comes new strength and new thoughts.

Eleanor Roosevelt

Resilience Training and How it Works

Resilience training is an increasingly common component of an overall wellness curriculum among residency programs and medical schools. It is founded on principles of positive psychology (the science behind positive subjective experiences, positive individual traits, and positive institutions[33]) and cognitive behavioral therapy (a process used in the treatment of depression, anxiety, and other chronic mental health problems to increase self-awareness of dysfunctional thinking).[22,34,35] Resilience skill-building is an evidence-based teachable set of behaviors, actions, and thoughts accessible to anyone—even residents and medical students facing the rigors of training.

The Resilience Toolkit

Recognizing and addressing inaccurate thought content is part of the toolkit for everyday stressors in post-graduate and graduate training. Resilience skill-building will teach you how to tap into your belief system and reframe your thinking to overcome adversities, bounce back from difficult times, and proactively reach your fullest potential. You will learn in-the-moment strategies for monitoring your thoughts, regulating negative feelings, and maintaining a sense of calm and self-esteem.

How Does Resilience Skill-Building Work?

An increasing number of residency programs and medical schools are offering opportunities for trainees to hone their resilience skills. Usually provided as individual skill-building activities and small-group workshops, resilience exercises seek to improve trainee coping skills as well as the quality of patient care. Group sessions are conducted in a safe environment, often facilitated by trained professionals.[22,35]

Building Self-Awareness

The resilience exercises are divided into two different subgroups: **You-Guru** and **You-Dini**.

- **You-Guru** is a self-study to explore your own mind, trying to really understand your deep-seated core beliefs and some of your thinking filters. If left unchecked, these can lead to inaccurate or distorted thinking.
- **You-Dini** is the learning and practice needed to escape some of your thinking traps.

Become a You-Guru

The Buddhist and Hindu traditions define a "guru" as a spiritual leader, a teacher who can show one the ways toward wisdom. Becoming a You-Guru requires something you already possess: curiosity. With curiosity, your You-Guru will build self-awareness along a journey of self-discovery. Your You-Guru teaches anatomy, but not the mastery of bone-to-bone articulations and locations of muscle insertions; these are facts you can probably recite in your sleep or readily access when needed. In achieving resilience, you are your own radiologist looking inward, becoming a learner and teacher at once, open to self-study in the ways of your own mind. The You-Guru learns what makes you happy, sad, and anxious, and learns your behaviors and thoughts day to day.

Deep-Seated Core Beliefs

Be open to learning about what makes your mind tick. This means learning how your automatic thoughts and your more deep-seated, core beliefs filter the way you process adversity and stressors.[24] As you learned in the last chapter, your belief filter is a kind of lens that may or may not be helpful in responding to what life throws at you. Whether the stressors come as difficulties on the wards or conflicts at home, your belief filter impacts the way you feel and how you act. This emotional/behavioral coping style can be resilient and helpful, or founded on false thinking that generates distressing feelings and maladaptive behaviors.

For many in healthcare, improving resilience requires shifting your point of view, changing your thinking filters to reduce distressing emotions and behaviors in response to adversity.[22] Like any behavioral change, changing your coping style is not easy and it takes practice.

You-Guru Exercises

The You-Guru exercises help you to understand your own thinking filters by having you take your cognitive vital signs. These exercises will help guide the more detailed paths of exploration:

- **Mind Pulse Exercise:** Get to know your stream of consciousness; this is a primer in self-awareness.
- **Emotional Temperature Exercise**: Determine your feelings at stressful moments and rate their intensity.
- **Thought X-Ray Exercise.** Learn common patterns of dysfunctional, unhelpful beliefs and behaviors in response to stressors to find the "fracture" or gaps. Your thought X-ray may reveal missing links between the truth and the reality of a given stressor. You will then be ready to fill in those gaps with the next set of exercises.

Become a You-Dini

Freeing Yourself From Thinking Traps

You may have heard of the magician and stunt performer Harry Houdini. You may even have seen video of him methodically, calmly, and almost effortlessly achieve death-defying feats: breaking chains and escaping submerged cages. In a sense, the You-Dini exercises will help you to unravel chains and pick locks so you, too, can metaphorically escape a submerged cage and triumphantly ascend to the surface to greet the gasping and adoring onlookers.

Your You-Dini chains are the thoughts, ways of thinking, habits, and coping skills which could contribute to your unhelpful beliefs. The way you think can form a cage or a sort of trap. Know that freeing yourself from thinking traps is no act of magic—it is hard work, because learning to change takes practice.

You-Dini Exercises

You-Dini exercises consist of:

- **Positive Evidence Points (PEP) Exercise**: Use a gaming approach to build self-esteem and obtain support from peers and mentors.
- **Thought-Balloon Exercise**: Counteract unhelpful beliefs with the aid of breathwork and visualization.
- **Nucleus Beliefs Exercise**: Detect deeply rooted beliefs of how you view yourself, others, the future, and the world.
- **Gaussian Distribution of the Mind Exercise**: Put into perspective the probability of an event actually occurring to help reduce anxiety.
- **Narrative Medicine Exercise**: Learn how narrative, or storytelling, can help you process emotions and cope with some of the toughest challenges in medicine.
- **Personal Mission Statement Exercise**: Define goals that can shape, mend, mold, and hold you steady on a path to maintain optimism.
- **Managing Conflicts Exercise**: Attain in-the-moment tools to help you build the capacity to cope with difficult feelings and practice emotional control.

- **Crash Cart Resilience Exercise**: Learn additional real-time tools to monitor your thinking and emotional responses to stressors and help you with impulse control.

We will review each of these exercises in the chapters that follow.

CHAPTER 5
MIND PULSE EXERCISE

The world as we have created it is a process of our thinking.
It cannot be changed without changing our thinking.

Albert Einstein

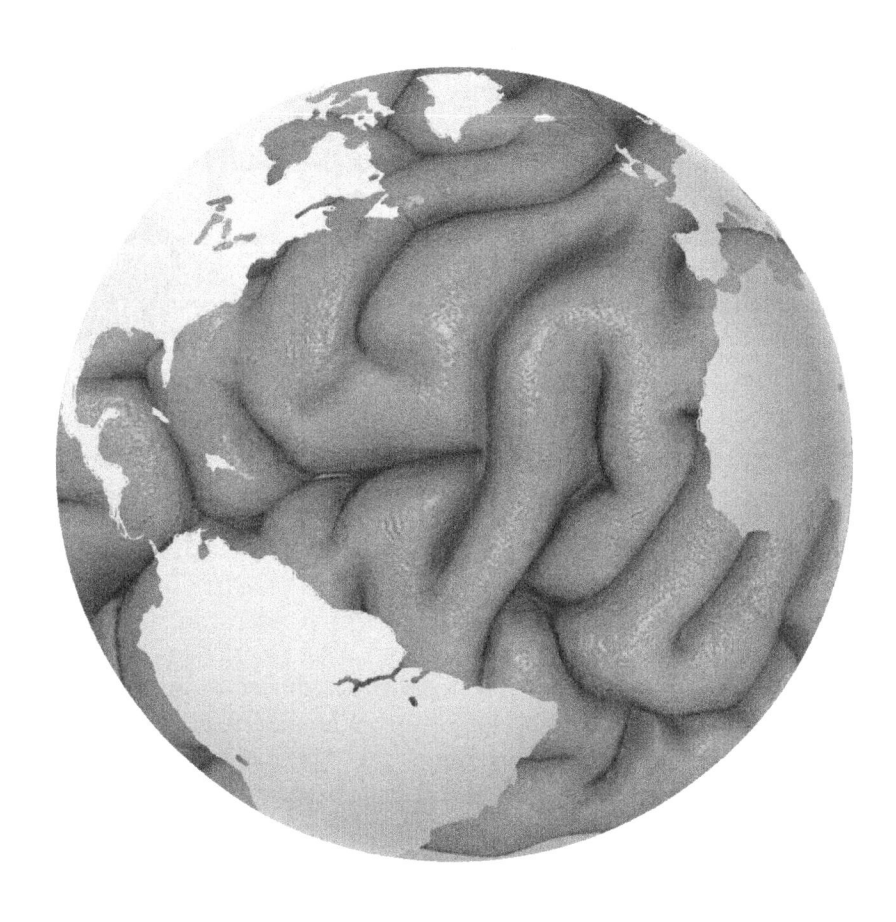

Objectives and Description

The Mind Pulse Exercise is an introduction to the way you think, and it is a first step toward mindfulness practice. Mind-pulse readings are a type of consciousness "vital sign" that will introduce you to how you think in a non-judgmental manner. The goal of this exercise is to reveal patterns useful for a deeper analysis in subsequent exercises.

Being mindful means paying attention, staying in the present moment, and remaining attentive to what is happening *around and within* you, including your thoughts and feelings. A key element of mindfulness is being non-judgmental—just accepting what crosses your consciousness when taking your mind pulse. Mindfulness is an underlying quality of wellness and resilience that is associated with physician well-being, career satisfaction, and positivity, and it correlates positively with quality patient care.[36]

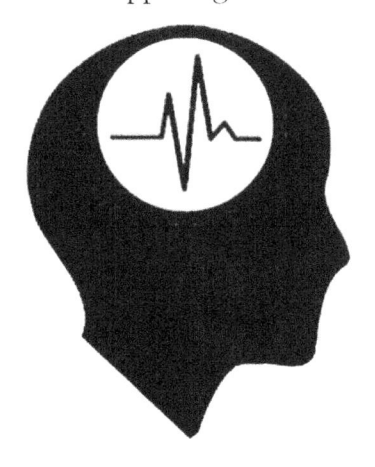

Mind Pulse Exercise Instructions

Random Pulse Checks

Set reminders on your smartphone or other device to go off *four to five random times each day for one week*. If you find it easier to set a reminder to go off at the same time each day, that's fine, provided that approach will help you to remember to do the exercise. However, it is preferable to take random pulses because you are more likely to record a range of observations.

Record Thoughts and Feelings, Not Actions

Write down your thoughts as if you are listening to a ticker tape of the thoughts running through your head. Be honest and don't hesitate, just write what comes to mind. Be open to your heart and mind, no matter what you are thinking or feeling. Difficult, neutral, and positive experiences are equally acceptable entries.

Avoid narrating what you are doing or recording sequential details of activity. That will not reveal useful information.

Let It Flow Naturally

Don't let this exercise interrupt your work or any clinical interactions. Whether working on the wards or seeing a patient in clinic, be mindful of strong emotions, take a mental note of what you are thinking during the patient-physician interaction, and write down your thoughts when it is convenient. This thoughtful delay is good practice for being self-aware while still going about your daily work.

Mind Pulse Examples

Below are examples of what a Mind Pulse log entry might look like.

Date	Time	What Was I Thinking?	What Was I Feeling?	What Was I Doing?
Mon.	2:10 pm	That patient seems angry with me. I don't think I can handle seeing this patient on a bad day! I tried my best but she had so many questions. I regret having to apologize for not answering her questions. She frowned, so I must have appeared clueless.	Embarrassed, regret, uncomfortable with myself.	Just saw a patient in continuity clinic.
Mon.	6:20 pm	This salad is so fresh! The hospital cafeteria here rocks. I am going to savor every bite.	Satisfied, appreciative.	Having dinner.

Worksheet

Use the Mind Pulse worksheet provided in this book. Alternatively, if you would like more space for your entries, prepare a separate form on your smartphone, laptop, or other device with columns labeled as follows:

Date	Time	What Was I Thinking?	What Was I Feeling?	What Was I Doing?

Mind Pulse Worksheet

Date	Time	What Was I Thinking?	What Was I Feeling?	What Was I Doing?
Day 1					
Day 2					
Day 3					

		Day 4		
		Day 5		
		Day 6		
		Day 7		

Analyze Your Results

You can stop recording your thoughts after one week, or you can continue until you become naturally aware of your stream of consciousness. Then analyze your mind pulse checks to see if there is a pattern. For example:

- **Assuming Negative Outcomes**: Are you thinking, "What if 'X' happens?"
- **Attributing Causes of Events or Situations**: This means we tend to find reasons and "whys" for things that happen.
- **Negative or Positive Outlooks**: Looking at situations generally negatively or positively.
- **Self-Referencing Themes**: How do I think of myself? (For example, as confident, autonomous, capable, self-blaming, guilty, shameful, regretful, etc.)

Use Your Results

Congratulations! You have taken an important step toward building resilience. You now have a set of data points into how your mind works, the kind of self-knowledge that will help you cope with adversity and stress. Resist judging yourself or being critical. Remember that this knowledge can only be helpful—being accepting and non-judgmental of what you've learned is equally important to the knowledge gained.

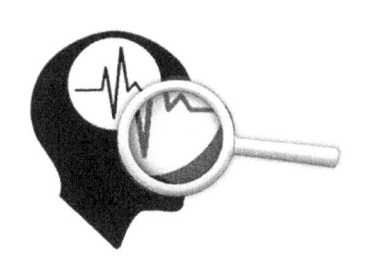

Now that you have acquired important self-knowledge that will help you cope with adversity and stress, don't stop here. This is a building block for other exercises and we will use this data as we work through the *CoreWellness* program.

Keep what you write to yourself private, unless you want to share some of your insights in a group wellness workshop or in private one-on-one counseling sessions.

CHAPTER 6
EMOTIONAL TEMPERATURE EXERCISE

> The highest possible stage in moral culture is when we recognize that we ought to control our thoughts.
>
> *Charles Darwin*

Objectives and Description

Residents and medical students find that this Emotional Temperature Exercise helps increase self-awareness of how adversities affect their emotions.[15] You will discover how certain events or stressors can trigger strong emotions in you. By using your own emotional thermometer, you will add to the self-knowledge you gained from the random mind pulse checks in the previous chapter. You will also find that more patterns emerge, and we will explore those in the other exercises.

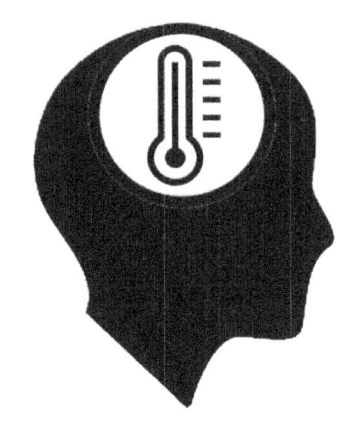

To determine your emotional temperature, you will fill out a brief log that relates stressors with the severity of your responses on a 0-5 point scale:
- 5 - very strong and need help dealing with feelings
- 4 - strong and somewhat distracting
- 3 - noticeable but not interfering
- 2 - slight, easily ignored
- 1 - barely noticeable
- 0 - neutral

Be open to taking these emotional temperatures when necessary—both inside and outside the clinical setting—when you are experiencing strong feelings. Why? Because, in addition to training-related stress, residents and medical students often experience strain within relationships during training.

As part of this exercise, you will identify when and where adversities and triggers happen (whether in the hospital, the classroom, or at home) and how you think about stressors in the moment and respond to them emotionally. This can help improve quality of life inside as well as outside the hospital.[3]

After filling out the Emotional Temperature Log you can review, analyze, and enhance self-awareness of the connections you are making between immediate thoughts/beliefs in response to adversity and the strong emotional responses that the thought content can evoke.

Addressing "Negative" Emotions

Sometimes people will refer to distressing emotions as negative. Remember that powerful feelings such as grief or sadness after a patient dies, and momentary anger in response to an attending's unreasonable criticism, are normal. The challenge is to hold back on first impulses, and to acknowledge these feelings as part of who you are without holding onto them. Retaining strong feelings and unhelpful beliefs associated with such emotions can lead to distress and difficulty functioning. This set of temperature readings is a deeper level of self-exploration whereby you will learn *how* you respond to and process adversities—insight that can help you avoid distress and burnout.

Emotional Temperature Exercise Instructions

When taking your Emotional Temperature you will use an emotion intensity score representing a validated emotions scale that is used in pediatrics. A similar scale is used in oncology for self-assessment of distress in cancer patients.[37] Emotion intensity scales are also used in different post-graduate educational settings as part of resilience training.[22]

There is no right or wrong way to monitor your emotions other than to have a consistent numerical grading score and to note negative emotions such as anger, anxiousness, or sadness. It is best to note only those that are *strong or intense*, as these feelings have the most potential to be distracting or problematic. Next to the intensity score, write down one or more emotions that you were experiencing at the time.

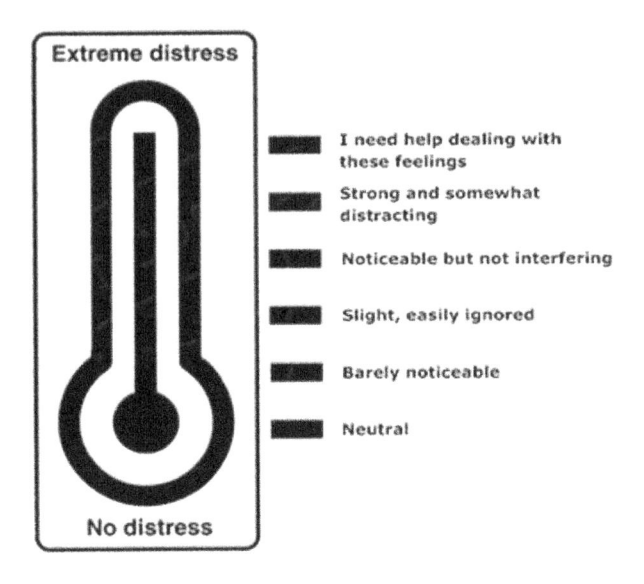

Extreme distress

- I need help dealing with these feelings
- Strong and somewhat distracting
- Noticeable but not interfering
- Slight, easily ignored
- Barely noticeable
- Neutral

No distress

Emotional Temperature Log

Create an Emotional Temperature Log with five columns labeled: Date/Time, Stressor, Emotion Type, Emotion Intensity, and Thoughts. (You can use the log provided at the end of this chapter, or create your own.) It is best to note only those that are strong or intense (emotion intensity of 4 or 5), as these feelings have the most potential to be distracting or problematic in some other way that you can describe. Next to the intensity score, be sure to pick one or more emotions you were experiencing at the time. Record for one week, or longer if you think it is necessary.

Date and Time to Collect Information

Unlike the random Mind Pulse exercise, you will take your Emotional Temperature when you are experiencing powerful feelings and emotions, noting the date and time. This can happen at any time, but a pattern may emerge.

Be guided by the Mind Pulse data to heighten your awareness of the kinds of adversities and stressors that spark strong, potentially distressing emotional responses. If the same episodes recur, take your emotional pulse. However, be open to other sources of stressors, both at work and when with family/friends.

Stressors

Record stressful situations in just a few words. Be factual. Avoid words that reflect emotions, opinions, or reactions. Save those kinds of descriptors for the Emotion Intensity column.

Examples of stressors might include:
- I did not finish pre-rounding on time for morning report.
- A barrage of pages/texts just came in from nursing staff with questions on clear, straightforward orders.
- I was not told on rounds about a patient with dementia who just pulled out her Foley.
- My colleague is late again to relieve me from the ED.
- I cannot find what I need for my patients during the first day at this community hospital because no one took the time to orient me.

These are a few of many example adversities related to training-associated stressors. Other more general stressors related to specific, difficult situations that you might record in your log include:
- transitions between rotations
- long working hours (frayed emotions post-call, difficulty coping with fatigue)
- feelings of isolation
- hostile working environment, harassment, or bullying

Outside of the training environment, be open to exploring other triggers such as:
- interpersonal difficulties with spouse or significant other
- finding work-life balance (finding time for family, doctor appointments)
- coping with a crisis within your family (death of loved one, illness, divorce/separation)
- financial concerns (filing taxes, repaying loans, dealing with debt)
- dealing with strains of a relationship

Thoughts

Use the log's "thoughts" column to write sentences similar to those you wrote during the Mind Pulse exercise. In one or two sentences, jot down your thoughts, not actions. You will begin the next exercise by reviewing this column with additional insight.

Analyze Your Results

After one week of logging, look for any patterns. Can you recognize ABC patterns? Remember your ABC model to help identify not only the A (adversity) and C (consequences), but also the extremely important underlying B's.

You may want to ask yourself the following questions to help interpret your responses and look for patterns:
- Do most of the scores indicate you need support for handling the feeling?
- Are many of the scores low?
- Does the intensity of emotions seem out of proportion to the stressor(s)?
- Are you feeling distressed by most of the strong feelings (e.g. do the feelings/reactions make you concerned more now that you are aware of them)?

- Did you have trouble articulating or finding words for your feelings?

Use Your Results

The Emotional Temperature Exercise is another resilience skill-building exercise best practiced in a supportive setting. Residency programs medical schools that have implemented resilience training find that emotional temperature self-assessments are one data set that improves self-efficacy, along with other resilience measures that reduce stress and risk for burnout.[22]

Emotional Temperature Worksheet

Date & Time	Stressor	Emotion Type	Emotion Intensity	Thoughts
		• Anger • Sadness • Disgust • Anxiousness • Surprise • Joy • Trust • Anticipation • Other _____	5 - Need help dealing with feelings 4 - Strong and somewhat distracting 3 - Noticeable but not interfering 2 - Slight, easily ignored 1 - Barely noticeable 0 - Neutral	
		• Anger • Sadness • Disgust • Anxiousness • Surprise • Joy • Trust • Anticipation • Other _____	5 - Need help dealing with feelings 4 - Strong and somewhat distracting 3 - Noticeable but not interfering 2 - Slight, easily ignored 1 - Barely noticeable 0 - Neutral	
		• Anger • Sadness • Disgust • Anxiousness • Surprise • Joy • Trust • Anticipation • Other _____	5 - Need help dealing with feelings 4 - Strong and somewhat distracting 3 - Noticeable but not interfering 2 - Slight, easily ignored 1 - Barely noticeable 0 - Neutral	

		• Anger • Sadness • Disgust • Anxiousness • Surprise • Joy • Trust • Anticipation • Other_____	5 - Need help dealing with feelings 4 - Strong and somewhat distracting 3 - Noticeable but not interfering 2 - Slight, easily ignored 1 - Barely noticeable 0 - Neutral	
		• Anger • Sadness • Disgust • Anxiousness • Surprise • Joy • Trust • Anticipation • Other _____	5 - Need help dealing with feelings 4 - Strong and somewhat distracting 3 - Noticeable but not interfering 2 - Slight, easily ignored 1 - Barely noticeable 0 - Neutral	
		• Anger • Sadness • Disgust • Anxiousness • Surprise • Joy • Trust • Anticipation • Other _____	5 - Need help dealing with feelings 4 - Strong and somewhat distracting 3 - Noticeable but not interfering 2 - Slight, easily ignored 1 - Barely noticeable 0 - Neutral	

Date & Time	Stressor	Emotion Type	Emotion Intensity	Thoughts
		• Anger • Sadness • Disgust • Anxiousness • Surprise • Joy • Trust • Anticipation • Other _____	5 - Need help dealing with feelings 4 - Strong and somewhat distracting 3 - Noticeable but not interfering 2 - Slight, easily ignored 1 - Barely noticeable 0 - Neutral	
		• Anger • Sadness • Disgust • Anxiousness • Surprise • Joy • Trust • Anticipation • Other _____	5 - Need help dealing with feelings 4 - Strong and somewhat distracting 3 - Noticeable but not interfering 2 - Slight, easily ignored 1 - Barely noticeable 0 - Neutral	

CHAPTER 7
THOUGHT X-RAY AND
–OMETER EXERCISES

The ancestor of every action is a thought.

Ralph Waldo Emerson

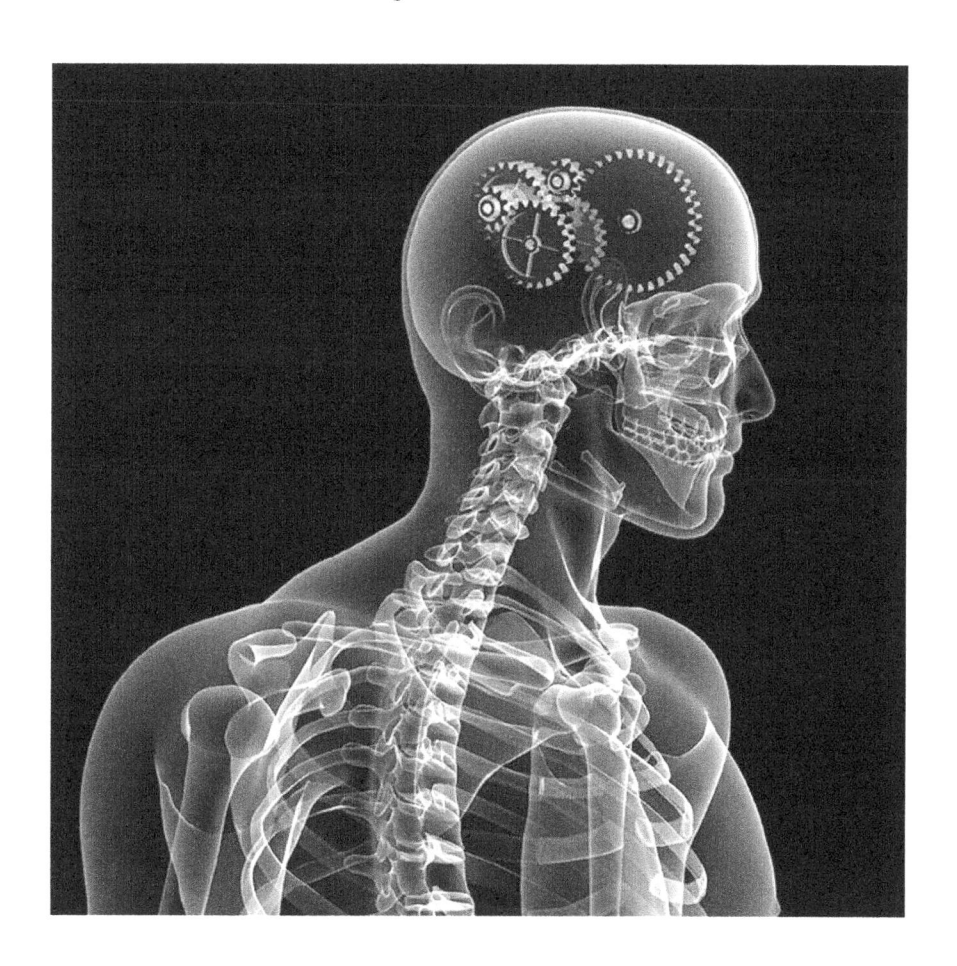

Objectives and Description

So far you have used data to look for gaps between the adversity/stressor and emotions and/or sets of beliefs. In the next exercise you will learn to recognize any gaps using a different type of journal consisting of Thought X-Ray Worksheets.

This is a self-discovery exercise to help you to take a deeper look into your thinking, like a radiologist studying a radiograph up close. Your notes will help you find one or more fractures—not osseous defects brought about by trauma or an underlying process, but an overly intense or counterproductive emotional/behavioral response generated by cognitive distortions.

Sometimes referred to as cognitive errors or cognitive distortions, these beliefs are not founded on fact and they often go unnoticed.[38] They happen in response to adversities that lead to unnecessarily strong feelings and even behaviors, and this type of thinking causes distress or seems out of proportion to the triggering adversity or stressor.

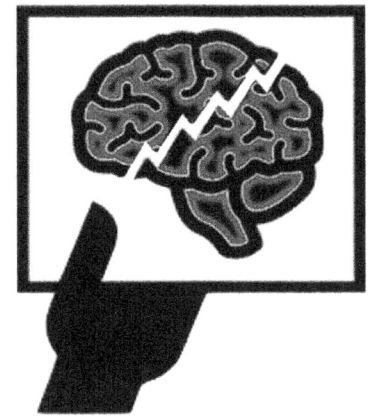

Cognitive distortion sounds worse than it is—they are quite common. *Dysfunctional thinking* is a cognitive behavioral therapy (CBT) term referring to beliefs many people carry around that could widen the gap between what is happening and how you would prefer to respond.

How do you know you have a thought/behavior fracture, or a thought distortion? If you are in any way distressed or somehow regret coping styles based on what you know so far from reviewing your Mind Pulse or Emotional Temperature exercises, then you have already uncovered a reason to change. Your distress means that it's time to look further inward and be open to change. Emotions are real and normal, but they need not be distressing.

This Thought X-Ray Exercise will help you discover the thinking traps and misguided beliefs common to all types of work environments, ones that may cause you to become stuck and feel distressed.

Strong Emotions

Keep in mind that strong emotions are not harmful. You most likely know this, but do you believe that statement? High emotional temperature vital signs are good signs, because they appear on your own log in your own words. These readings prove that you are emotionally aware.

Rather than feel distressed by the reality of strong emotions, take a moment to congratulate yourself for taking a big You-Guru step that will continue to help build resilience. Remember, the goal here is not to numb or negate strong emotions, but to help process them and to take the next step toward self-awareness by understanding the thinking that contributed to those emotions.

Because residency and medical school are intense, high temperature scores are to be expected. If they happen multiple times, that may mean you need to find support, especially in the face of tragedy, such as losing a patient you tried hard to save. Your Thought X-Ray Worksheet may include such an extreme circumstance or something similar, resulting in distressing emotions like grief. The grieving process is normal. However, strong emotions after such an adversity can creep up on you again and again if you do not process the experience based on helpful, evidenced-based thoughts.

Grounding in Reality

Your Thought X-Ray could include thought content in response to such tragedy such as, "I caused the patient's death because I did not act quickly enough or try hard enough." These thoughts are not going to help you. They represent guilt and self-blame that can hold you back.

In the Thought X-ray Exercise, you will learn examples of thought content that could be helpful, healing, and resilience-building. Belief and faith in yourself as a hard-working but fallible healer is reflected in thought content such as, "I tried my best," "Patients sometimes die despite best efforts," or "I can get through this." These thoughts are truths, not distortions, accepting our fallibility as healers, and founded on self-compassion. It is important to recognize that helpful thought content doesn't remove the pain of adversities, but it does help you cope with powerful emotions that are grounded in reality.

Thought X-Ray Exercise Instructions

Use the Thought X-Ray Worksheet provided on the next page, or make one of your own so you can record the following:

- stressor/adversity
- your thoughts
- your feelings
- what you were doing

Upon experiencing the adversity, or at a convenient time afterward, fill in the worksheet sections. Complete a set of thought X-rays over one week, and make several entries into your Thought X-Ray Worksheet each day. The worksheet will remind you that an adversity (A) gives rise to thoughts/beliefs (B) that contribute to emotional and behavioral responses—the consequence (C).

A → B → C

Thought X-Ray Worksheet

	Describe the Stressor or Adversity	What Are Your Thoughts in Response to the Stressor or Adversity?	What Are Your Feelings and Are They Intense? (Emotional Temperature Rating 0- 5)	What Are You Doing? Describe Behaviors at the Time of the Stressor or Adversity
1				
2				
3				
4				
5				
6				
7				
8				
9				
10				

	Describe the Stressor or Adversity	What Are Your Thoughts in Response to the Stressor or Adversity?	What Are Your Feelings and Are They Intense? (Emotional Temperature Rating 0- 5)	What Are You Doing? Describe Behaviors at the Time of the Stressor or Adversity
11				
12				
13				
14				
15				
16				

Thought and Behavior Patterns

Here is where you will recognize that beliefs and thoughts in response to adversities come in familiar patterns. Some lead to resilient behavior while others lead to distress. The reason for the wide variation becomes apparent when comparing how your peers react to the same stressors. Everyone is wired differently with respect to coping and thinking patterns in handling adversity. Recognition of your thinking style will help you to understand how the B's may enable you to react more calmly and with clarity in response to the same pressures when compared with your colleagues. As you work through this exercise, you will also gain insight as to why the converse is true.

However, taking your thought X-ray is not a competitive sport. This exercise is not about reaching perfect states of calm under pressure. The purpose is to learn about yourself and help support your peers. You can achieve this dual goal by answering "yes" or "no" in the columns and by beginning to understand the nuances of your coping styles. As you put the spotlight on your own ABC's, you will begin to capture and record your personal B's while also acquiring insight into the nature of thoughts and beliefs that help or hinder your resilience.

The patterns of A to B to C that you uncover might demonstrate emotions or behaviors (consequences) that cause distress or somehow impair your ability to cope with adversity. Maladaptive emotions and behaviors can follow factual errors in beliefs, patterns of thinking that could erode resilience and increase the risk for burnout, anxiety, or depression.[22,24]

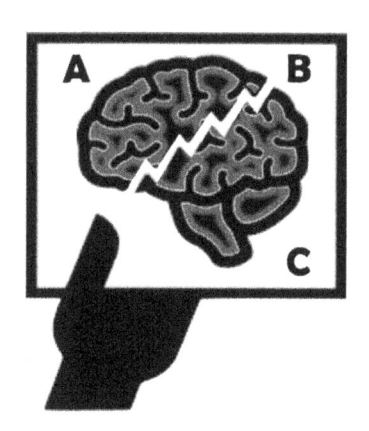

The –Ometer Exercise

Review any evidence of dysfunctional thinking and unhelpful behavior patterns when filling in the "-Ometer" columns on the worksheet below, answering "Yes" or "No."

	TRUTH-OMETER (Are my thoughts or beliefs true?)	**EMOTION-OMETER** (Does my emotional response seem appropriate to the stressor/adversity?)	**HELP-OMETER** (Is my behavior(s) helping me cope?)
1	Yes No	Yes No	Yes No
2	Yes No	Yes No	Yes No
3	Yes No	Yes No	Yes No
4	Yes No	Yes No	Yes No
5	Yes No	Yes No	Yes No
6	Yes No	Yes No	Yes No
7	Yes No	Yes No	Yes No
8	Yes No	Yes No	Yes No
9	Yes No	Yes No	Yes No

10	Yes No	Yes No	Yes No
11	Yes No	Yes No	Yes No
12	Yes No	Yes No	Yes No
13	Yes No	Yes No	Yes No
14	Yes No	Yes No	Yes No
15	Yes No	Yes No	Yes No
16	Yes No	Yes No	Yes No

Review Your Worksheets

Check Your Yes's and No's Each Day

At the end of each day or another specified time, review your Thought X-Ray and –Ometer worksheets. Again, here is what you should think about, both at the time (or close to the time) of the stressor and after a few hours:

- **Truth-ometer**: Are my thoughts/beliefs true?
- **Emotion-ometer**: Do the emotions and emotional intensities seem appropriate to the stressor/adversity?
- **Behavior-ometer:** Are my behaviors helping me cope?

Complete Your Final Review at the End of the Week

After you have filled out a week of Thought X-Ray Worksheets, determine whether you have identified "No's" which could point to fractures or gaps between the adversity (A) and the consequences (C), the emotions or behaviors resulting from unhelpful beliefs (B). You can then determine not only if you have "No's" but also have the self-knowledge to identify the types of beliefs that may interfere with resilience. If several stressors during the week give rise to false beliefs and unhelpful behaviors, do not despair—there are many alternative ways of viewing even the most challenging of situations!

Dysfunctional Thinking

Imagine your own thought/behavior radiograph. If you answered "No" in the columns, there could be cognitive fractures, or gaps, between the stressor and your beliefs. In other words, your thinking may not be founded in truth, but rather be based on established patterns. These may be emotions or behaviors that impair your coping ability in response to the stressor and which undermine your resilience.

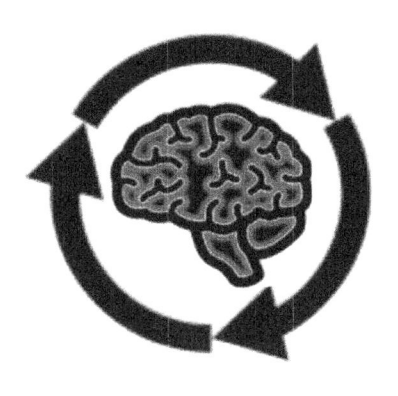

These dysfunctional thinking traps can be categorized into two groups: automatic thoughts and core beliefs.[24]

Automatic Thoughts

Automatic thoughts are situation-specific thinking traps that go under the radar of awareness, containing reflexive self-appraisals, assessments of the immediate stressor, and beliefs about the stressor/adversity's impact on your future. The table below provides definitions, examples, and ways to avoid the different types of thinking traps.

Definition	Example	Avoiding Thinking Traps
Jumping to Conclusions: Believing something when there is little or no evidence to support it.	"My program director left me a voice message to call her right away. I must have done something wrong."	Ask yourself to make a concerted effort to accurately look at the facts and weigh the evidence before making conclusions.
Emotional Reasoning: Making the assumption that, in the face of adversity, your emotions are always accurate indicators of the nature of the adversity.	"I feel guilty my patient is displeased with the diet I ordered for her. I must have done something wrong."	Separate your feelings from your judgment. Ask yourself if you have an accurate view about the situation if you ignore your feelings. Sometimes it is best to reevaluate the situation after your feelings have subsided.
Magnifying and Minimizing: Exaggerating the importance of certain aspects of a situation and diminishing others.	"Everyone told me that I did really well in my grand rounds presentation, but that does not mean I am a good speaker."	Ask yourself if you are overvaluing some components of a situation and undervaluing others.
Tunnel Vision: Having blinders or being unaware of the most important information about a situation, and instead focusing on insignificant details.	"I was asked a lot of good questions during and after my lecture, but one resident seemed disinterested. My lecture must have been really boring."	Ask yourself if you have made an accurate and fair assessment of the situation. Make sure you focus on the big picture and look objectively at a situation, and that you are not ignoring important information that can disconfirm your beliefs.

	Definition	Example	Avoiding Thinking Traps
Mind Reading:	Assuming that you know what another person is thinking, or expecting another person to know what you are thinking.	"I wanted to study for my test, but one of my classmates just kept talking to me. She should have known I did not want to talk."	Ask yourself if you are communicating well. Ask the other person a question that will help clarify where the communication breakdown has occurred.
Overgeneralizing:	Making broad assumptions, usually about lack of worth of yourself or others, based on very specific evidence.	"I just saw my USMLE Step 1 score and I am very disappointed. I don't know why I study so hard. I will always get poor grades."	Ask yourself if there a more specific explanation than the very general one you chose.
Personalizing:	The tendency to automatically attribute the cause of an adversity to one's personal characteristics or actions. This is the opposite of externalizing.	"The patient I took care of in clinic was admitted. I must have failed to provide adequate preventative care."	Ask yourself if you see only your contribution to the situation, but not the contributions of others. If so, what was their contribution?
Externalizing:	The tendency to automatically attribute the cause of an adversity to another person or to circumstances. This is the opposite of personalizing.	"The patient I took care of in clinic was admitted. I know I provided excellent care. Another resident must have failed to provide adequate preventative care."	Ask yourself if you see only others' contributions to a situation, but not your own. If so, what was your contribution?
"Musting" and "Shoulding":	Overly inflexible ideas or expectations of others or of oneself.	"I should not have to ask the attending to demonstrate surgical suturing more than once, or I will be perceived as incompetent."	Ask yourself if you can be more flexible regarding ideas or expectations.

Definition	Example	Avoiding Thinking Traps
All-or-Nothing Thinking: Viewing situations on one extreme or another instead of on a continuum.	"I want to the gym to work out, but I can't go every day. I might as well not go at all."	Ask yourself if you are viewing a situation in black and white. Are there any gray areas you should consider?
Catastrophizing: Assuming the worse possible outcome rather than positive or neutral ones.	"Because I was late for this morning's lecture, I will fail the clinical rotation and will have to drop out of medical school."	Ask yourself if you have a tendency to be anxious and focused on future threats.
Disqualifying or Discounting the Positive: Telling yourself that the good things that happen to you don't count.	"During rounds, my colleague told me that I was really helpful in admitting the last patient, but I'm sure she was just being polite."	Ask yourself if you are automatically discounting the good things that happen.
Labeling: Assessing someone's character generally, using an umbrella term, based on one instance of a behavior.	"The attending looked down during my presentation; he is so inconsiderate."	Ask yourself if you have enough evidence to suggest that a behavior can be attributed to a person's general character.

Core Beliefs

Core beliefs are deep-seated, pervasive beliefs that usually operate in several life areas, including at work and with family or friends. They are established during childhood and are reinforced with experience.[28]

Core beliefs can be classified into several self-schemas around themes including abandonment, defectiveness, incompetence, lack of self-control, and self-sacrifice.

Schema/Description	Schema-Associated Thought Snippets
Abandonment: A belief that people are unreliable, unstable, and not consistently available for support.	"I worry that people close to me will leave me." "I tend to cling to the people closest to me." "I feel desperate when I sense that someone I care about is rejecting me."
Defectiveness: Pervasive feelings and beliefs of inferiority and/or being unwanted. It tends toward hypersensitivity to criticism, self-blame, and insecurity around others.	"I don't belong." "I am a loner." "I feel like an outsider when I'm in a group."
Incompetence: Consistently requiring considerable help from others owing to pervasive self-doubt about one's ability to make independent decisions and actions.	"I am incompetent and have achieved very little in my life." "I am not as intelligent as most people." "I am not as talented as most people with whom I work." "My judgment is not reliable."
Lack of Self-Control: Having a low threshold for withholding expression of strong emotions, leading to avoidance of confrontation, responsibility, or new challenges.	"Unless I am in control, I am unhappy." "I am too sensitive." "It is dangerous for me to express my feelings." "I cannot take on too much responsibility or I will be overwhelmed." "I must avoid confrontations or risk losing my temper and being embarrassed."
Self-Sacrifice: An over-focus on meeting the needs of others for fear of being considered selfish, characterized by an acute sensitivity to another's pain and suffering.	"I am a good person because I think of others first." "I find little time to take care of myself because I am so busy taking care of others." "People see me as doing too much for others."

Unhelpful Behaviors

Unhelpful behaviors may or may not follow from dysfunctional thinking and emotional responses. In this exercise you only describe them, for example, "I avoided the most difficult patient and ended up rounding on him last," or, "I clenched my fists when the stat labs were late." You will have the opportunity to analyze both the beliefs and behaviors in the next step.

Now recognize that they come in two forms: somatic (only you notice them) and overt (actions/reactions that may be apparent to others). Examples include:
- **Somatic**: clenched fists, more rapid breathing, sweating.
- **Overt**: avoidance of social contact, skipping meals, working more than necessary, procrastination, lashing out (angry remarks).

Somatic behaviors could be quite subtle, such as slight trembling or tightening of a muscle group. These behaviors are related to the response to adversity and, if they are accompanied by distressing feelings, represent difficulty coping.

Research on posttraumatic stress indicates that these maladaptive behaviors are learned over time and can be replaced with more helpful coping styles conducive to resilience.[26] For example, if you find that you react more somatically, breathing awareness may be most helpful in developing a more resilient coping style.[24]

Retrofit Your Emotional Thermometer

Now you will review a previous exercise, making the Emotional Temperature data even more valuable for you. This will help you recognize the adversity/stressor → beliefs/thoughts → emotions/behavior patterns.

1. Read the list of irrational beliefs again.
2. Make post-it notes of the types of beliefs that come to mind when handling adversities and stressors.
3. Go back to your Emotional Temperature Log and place an irrational belief post-it that most closely matches the kind of thinking that characterizes the "thoughts" column. No need to use paper or pen-pad; adapt this and all the exercises for your device of choice, or simply write over the notes you took in the "thoughts" column. See the example below.

Date & Time	Stressor	Emotion Type	Emotion Intensity	Thoughts
May 4th at 5 20 pm.	After presenting a patient to my attending on service he said I completely missed the most likely diagnosis for a patient.	☐ Anger ■ Sadness ☐ Disgust ☐ Anxiousness ☐ Surprise ☐ Joy ☐ Trust ☐ Anticipation ☐ Other	• 5 - Need help dealing with feelings ○ 4 - Strong and somewhat distracting ○ 3 - Noticeable but not interfering ○ 2 - Slight, easily ignored ○ 1 - Barely noticeable ○ 0 - Neutral	I really messed up. I must not be very intelligent *Incompetent*

CHAPTER 8
POSITIVE EVIDENCE POINTS EXERCISE

With realization of one's own potential
and self-confidence in one's ability,
one can build a better world.

Dalai Lama

Objectives and Description

In this exercise you will use a gaming approach to treat any thought fractures identified on your Thought X-ray Worksheet. The Positive Evidence Points (PEP) exercise is based on resilience training and will focus on techniques to build self-esteem.[22,39]

The overall objective of this exercise is to earn "positive evidence points" in the form of Evidence Cards, which contain brief statements in the following categories:
- **Affirmations**: positive, self-affirming statements.
- **Cheers**: positive feedback from colleagues, faculty preceptors, and career mentors.
- **Experience**: successful completion of new skills, accomplishments, or benchmark achievements such as admitting more patients and supervising junior residents.

In other words, we want you to **ACE** (Affirmations, Cheers, Experience) your PEP exercise.

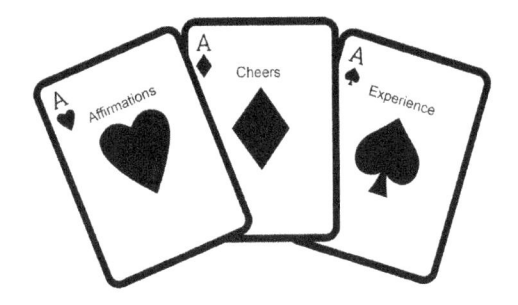

Cognitive Re-Ossification

The more points you earn, the weaker unhelpful thinking and core beliefs become while your self-confidence, self-efficacy, and sense of competence grow stronger. The way you process stressors can improve as you collect accurate real-world evidence; the evidence you accumulate will eventually give you the insight that adversities do not directly lead to consequences. This will result in a change in perspective, or a kind of cognitive re-ossification, as you intentionally bridge gaps between an adversity/stressor and emotions/behavior, decreasing your sense of distress and increasing your resilience.

You-Guru and You-Dini

Like the You-Guru worksheets with which you acquired essential self-knowledge, this PEP exercise will give you the chance to be a You-Dini by using insights to free yourself from the chains of dysfunctional beliefs and heal cognitive fractures based on evidence, experience, and support from your mentors and peers.

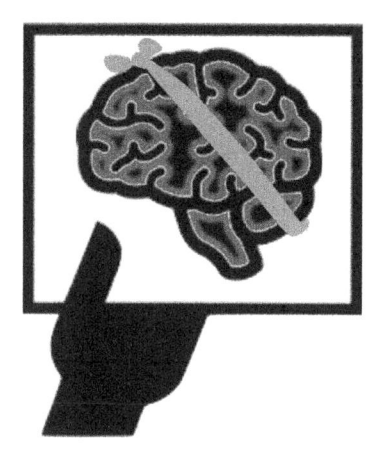

The PEP Exercise is a reward in itself. The very process of developing self-value appraisals builds awareness of your resilience. You become an automatic winner simply by participating in the exercise. Each day is a carpe-diem, a chance to seize the day! You will see your evidence vault fill up as you collect PEPs that help you win resilience day by day and during your upcoming rotations.

Cognitive Restructuring

Now that you have noticed how unhelpful thoughts cause a disconnect, or fracture, between adversity (the stressors) and its consequence (your emotions and behavior), you are ready to be your own orthopedist. You don't need plaster for molding a cast or sophisticated hardware to perform internal fixation, but you will require multiple methods of restructuring. You will design your own approach to remodel your thinking. All you need are three elements to get started:
1. ACE (Affirmations, Cheers, Experience) evidence cards
2. value appraisal, a self-assessed value of the evidence being collected
3. evidence "vault," a safe place to collect your evidence and store the PEPs

Remember, there are no winners or losers in this process. There are only the benefits you will gain by bolstering your self-esteem and competence.

The underlying cognitive behavioral intervention here, known as *cognitive restructuring*, has proven effective in reducing burnout risk and enhancing resilience in several work settings including residency.[7] Also known as reframing, or challenging, thoughts and beliefs, cognitive restructuring is the behavioral activation of CBT and is what you will actually be doing in the PEP exercise. The game may resemble some other fun activities you are doing as part of resilience skill-building within residency and medical school training. Like those other activities, the PEP exercise will challenge your maladaptive thoughts and beliefs with your own counter-positive statements, enhancing resilience and reducing stress.[24]

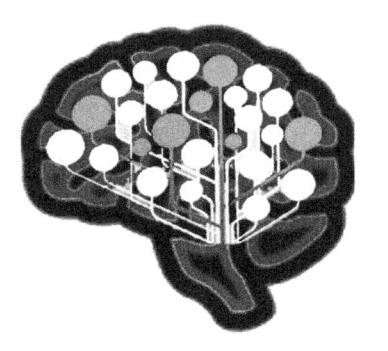

PEP Exercise Instructions

What you will need:
- resilience questionnaire
- ACE evidence cards
- point system
- evidence "vault"

Connor-Davidson Scale

Start with a pre-exercise resilience questionnaire to assess your baseline. We suggest you use the two-question version of Connor-Davidson Scale (CD-RISC2).[40] This is a shortened version of the CD-25 and CD-10 with only two questions that you would score before the PEP Exercise for a rough measure of resilience. (Note that you can replace the CD-RISC2 with another validated resilience or stress assessment.)

Using a rating scale from 0 to 4 (where 0=not at all, 1=sometimes, 2=about half the time, 3=most of the time, and 4=nearly all the time), determine how much the following questions apply to you:

Question	Score (0-4)
1. Are you able to adapt to change?	
2. Do you tend to bounce back after hardship?	
Total Score*	
*higher scores correspond to higher resilience	

Take the same CD-RISC2 Resilience Questionnaire after one month and then again every three to six months to assess your resilience progress.

ACE Evidence Cards

Once you've completed your resilience questionnaire, it is time to fill out written descriptions of evidence to challenge any dysfunctional or negative thinking. To do this, use the ACE cards provided on the next pages, or small index cards or e-equivalents of the cards created on your smartphone or another device. Each card will be assigned a point value. The three types of ACE cards are:

- **Affirmation Cards:** simple declarative sentences, written in your own words, to challenge negative automatic thoughts or core beliefs. The affirmations can also be general expressions of "can-do" confidence-building statements.
- **Cheers Cards:** summaries of supportive comments or recognition of successes from peers and positive feedback from mentors, as well as those you provide to colleagues or fellow students. It's ok to paraphrase or directly quote (such as from rotation evaluations).
- **Experience Cards:** summaries of procedures and skills (e.g. suturing, knot tying, lumbar puncture, thoracentesis, laparoscopy, etc.) that parallel your progress through medical school or residency. Be sure to include separate experience cards for supervising or teaching the same skill if these types of reinforcements bolster your sense of competence.

Recording your ACE evidence cards and the act of accumulating PEP provide real-world proof to negate unhelpful thinking. This resilience-building activity, which involves behavioral activation, can be quite helpful as you move through training. Again, you will assess the value of each ACE card based on how much each type of evidence (or support) builds resilience. Some people respond more to oral feedback, others to experience, or both. Affirmations go a long way to counter negative thinking, too.

Point System

Self-assign point values to determine how much each type of evidence is worth, using a scale of 1 (least valuable) to 10 (most valuable), and place the point value on the back of each evidence card. Only you know how valuable a given experience is for building your competence and resilience. For example, for you it could be that experience doing a new type of procedure has a value of 8 points, while teaching, supervising and observing proficiency in junior residents is worth 10 points.

A
♥ Affirmations

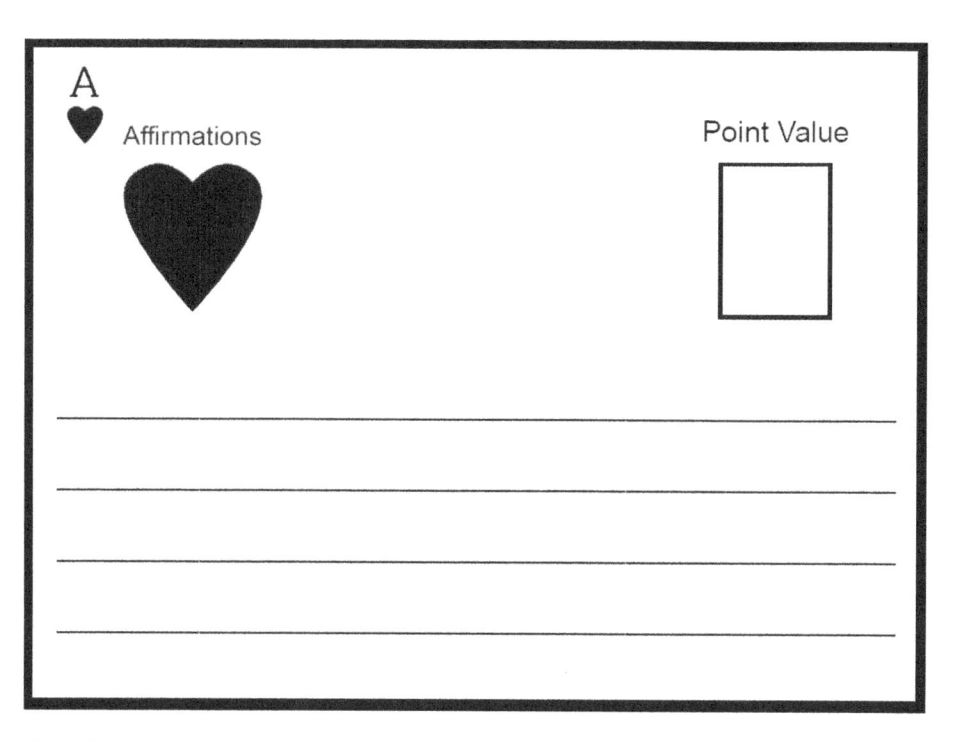

Point Value

A
♥ Affirmations

Point Value

A
♦ Cheers   Point Value

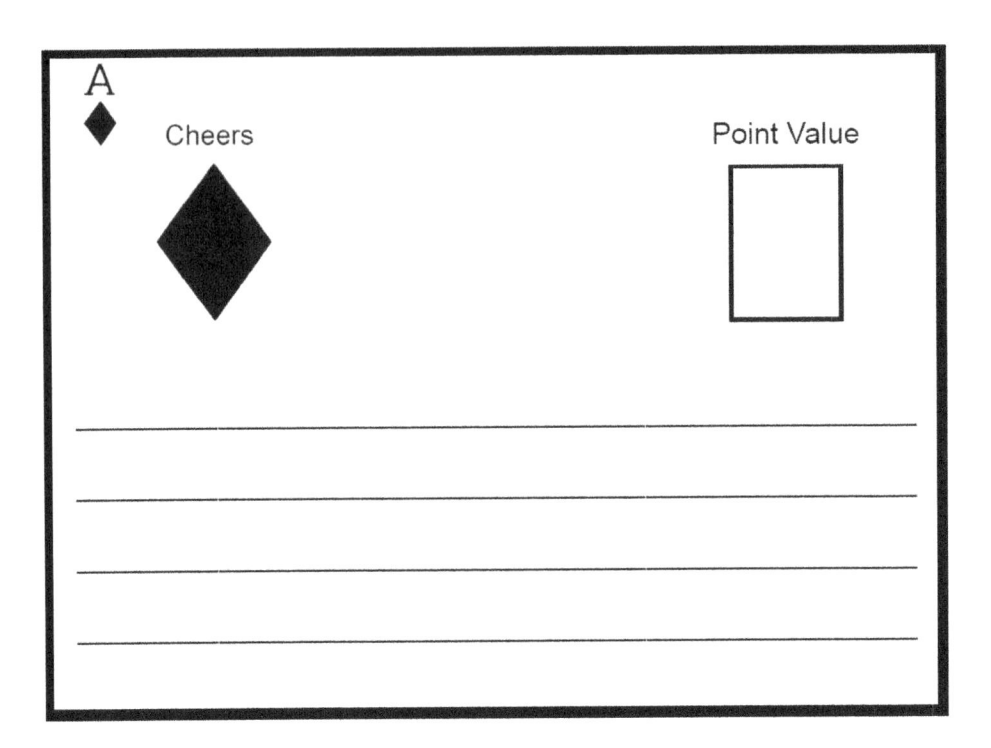

A
♦ Cheers   Point Value

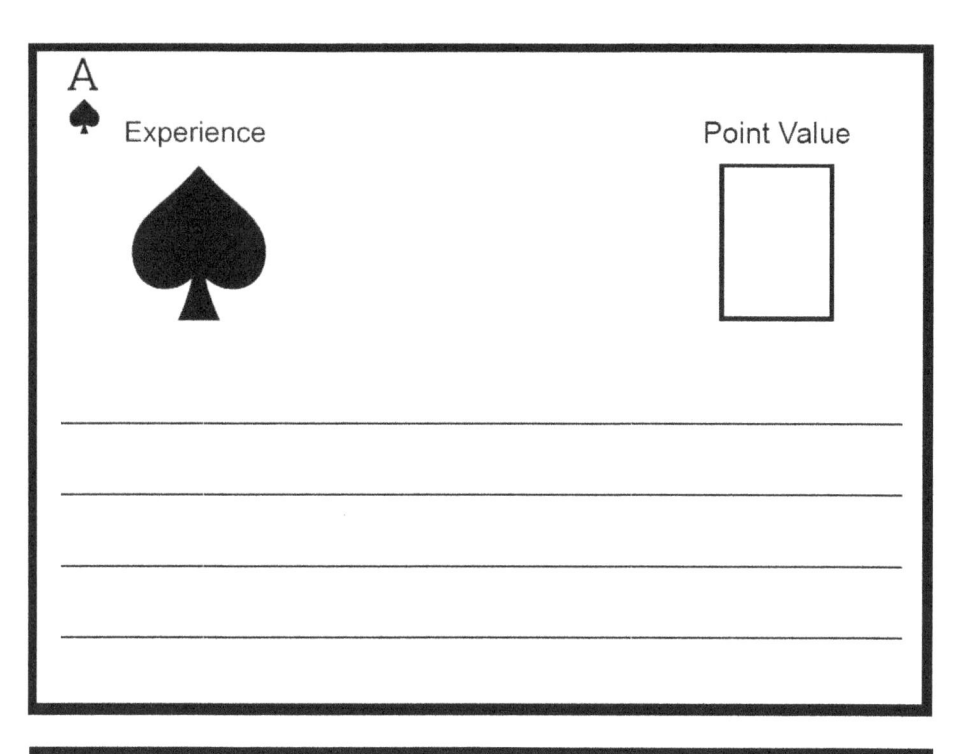

A ♠ Experience	Point Value

_____
_____
_____
_____

A ♠ Experience	Point Value

_____
_____
_____
_____

Evidence Vault

Designate an actual box, physical container, or virtual "e-box" for storing your ACE cards and PEP score sheet. The total value for the evidence cards should equal the scorecard tally on your PEP score sheet.

The PEP Score Sheet

Keep some ACE cards with you so you can record a positive evidence event (Affirmation, Cheers, Experience) right after it occurs, if feasible. Then transfer the information from the evidence card onto your PEP score sheet, using the one provided in this book or on your own electronic spreadsheet. Include the date and type of positive evidence that corresponds to the evidence cards you have been accumulating. Then tally the points every week as you accumulate positive evidence.

On the next page is a sample PEP Score Sheet showing a week of evidence.

Now it is your turn to gather evidence on the positive evidence cards and fill in the PEP score sheet at the end of this chapter with your own PEP and ACE.

Date	Positive Evidence	Affirmation	Cheers	Experience	# Points
11/21	Did my first full procedure "X" without any errors or complications.			X	8
11/21	I admitted 10 patients and wrote orders faster and more efficiently than I have ever done before.			X	7
11/22	I showed great emotion regulation when one of the faculty yelled at me for something that was not my fault.	X			9
11/23	I really enjoyed supervising a junior resident and teaching her an important new skill.			X	10
11/23	A nurse told me I did an excellent job explaining the diagnosis and management plan to a patient.		X		7
11/24	A faculty member that I consider a mentor told me I did a great job preparing and delivering a lecture to the department.		X		10
11/25	Doing presentations is getting so much easier for me and I am not even nervous anymore.	X			8
	WEEK TOTAL				59

Analyze and Use Your Results

Read and re-read your evidence cards. Hear the words of your colleagues, mentors, and faculty. Hear your own words describing all the procedures you have accomplished. Listen to your affirmations, too. Read your cards aloud.

Reinforce your successes. Challenge negative thinking and build resilience by counting your PEPs and noting how your score sheet totals are adding up.

PEP Score Sheet

Date	Positive Evidence	Affirmation	Cheers	Experience	# Points
	WEEK 1 TOTAL:				

	WEEK 2 TOTAL:				
	WEEK 3 TOTAL:				

	WEEK 4 TOTAL:			
	GRAND TOTAL (ALL WEEKS):			

CHAPTER 9:
THOUGHT-BALLOON EXERCISE

Breathe. Let go. And remind yourself that this very moment is the only one you know you have for sure.

Oprah Winfrey

Objectives and Description

This is a thought exercise for challenging unhelpful beliefs with work and visualization. All you need to do is imagine a stream, a balloon, and to breathe. Mindfulness techniques, including this exercise, help you focus on the present without being led astray by unhelpful thoughts or emotions from the past or about the future.

The objective of this exercise is to control your thoughts and let unhelpful or distressing thoughts go.

Controlling Your Thoughts

Breathing at the Center

Breathwork is at the heart of this and other mind-body and mindfulness exercises because the sensation of breathing is a readily accessible focal point. It is capable of anchoring you in the present and it is also conducive to relaxation.[24]

The Power of Imagination

As a child, did you ever hold a helium balloon and then let it go? Perhaps you were at the circus, walking out of a ballpark, or attending a friend's backyard birthday party when you felt the soft white twine tickle your fingers as the balloon began its ascent. What a delightful spectacle, uplifting your spirits, as you watched the balloon rise up toward the clouds!

In this exercise, you'll make your thoughts lighter than air. Think of the helium inside the balloon as your unhelpful thoughts or core beliefs. Whatever unique approach to this letting-go exercise works for you, be ready to try and try again, because it's not easy to let go of familiar thought patterns.

Thought-Balloon Exercise Instructions

Consciously Letting Go

Imagine that a strong gust of wind comes along and steals a helium balloon from a child, catching her by surprise. Maybe the child cries and makes one reflexive reach upward to grab the prized possession, but it's too late. Upward goes the red balloon despite the child's desire to hang onto it a bit longer.

Visualize creating your own red balloon, one that can be taken by the wind. You are in control of what thinking you need to keep and which dysfunctional thoughts and beliefs you want to let go. See yourself filling that balloon, breathing out your dysfunctional thoughts to make the balloon buoyant and ready to fly.

Now you have a choice: you decide where and when to let go of your red thought-balloon. When you are ready, imagine letting it go. Identify with the red balloon as it takes flight. The balloon's ascent is your freedom from dysfunctional beliefs, conferring a feeling of buoyancy and soaring—and increasing your resiliency.

Freeing Your Thought-Balloons

Step 1: Hear
When you feel strong emotions or when something stressful is happening, simply hear the stream of your thinking, be aware of the thought-stream, and imagine that it is a brook. Acknowledge that unhelpful thought-content is present but resist the temptation to listen and judge. Say to yourself, "I know these thoughts are not helping me, they are just trickling by in this little stream."

Step 2: Let Go

Now focus your attention on your imaginary balloon. You have the power to let go of your thoughts at will, just as you listened to them as a trickle down the stream. When you are ready, make the conscious decision to let the thoughts go, rising in your thought-balloon. Imagine the feel of the twine passing upward through your hand as the balloon ascends. In one or two seconds, feel the last gentle tickle of twine as its end leaves your hand, feel the moment you *let go of your thought balloon*. Imagine the balloon rising higher and higher, taking your thoughts with it.

Step 3: Breathe and Stay Grounded

Use your breathing to focus your attention on the sensation of air slowly going through your nose, noticing the passage of air filling your lungs. Exhale deeply, letting air leave your lungs. If you are seated, notice the back of the chair against your back. If standing, notice your feet touching the floor or ground. This is how you focus on the present moment while the balloon continues to rise out of view.

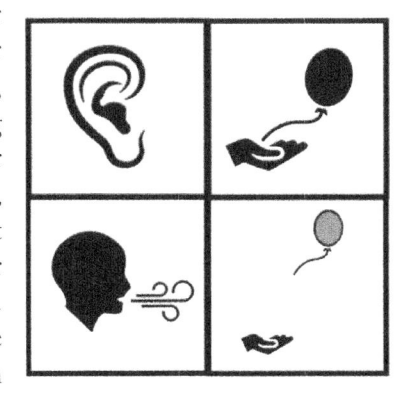

Step 4: Breathe and Let Go Again

The mind often wanders, and it may be doing so during this exercise. If this happens and unhelpful thoughts return, focus on the balloon again. Imagine that it misses you and is having a hard time taking off: the string may descend and try to tickle your fingers, as though asking you to open your hand and hold onto the twine again. You will not let your unhelpful thoughts return. Instead, focus on your breathing again. One slow inhalation and exhalation is all it takes to send the balloon aloft once more, up into the clouds forever. This is a beautiful sight, and you are left feeling more relaxed, in control, and resilient.

CHAPTER 10
NUCLEUS BELIEFS EXERCISE

Don't find fault. Find a remedy.

Henry Ford

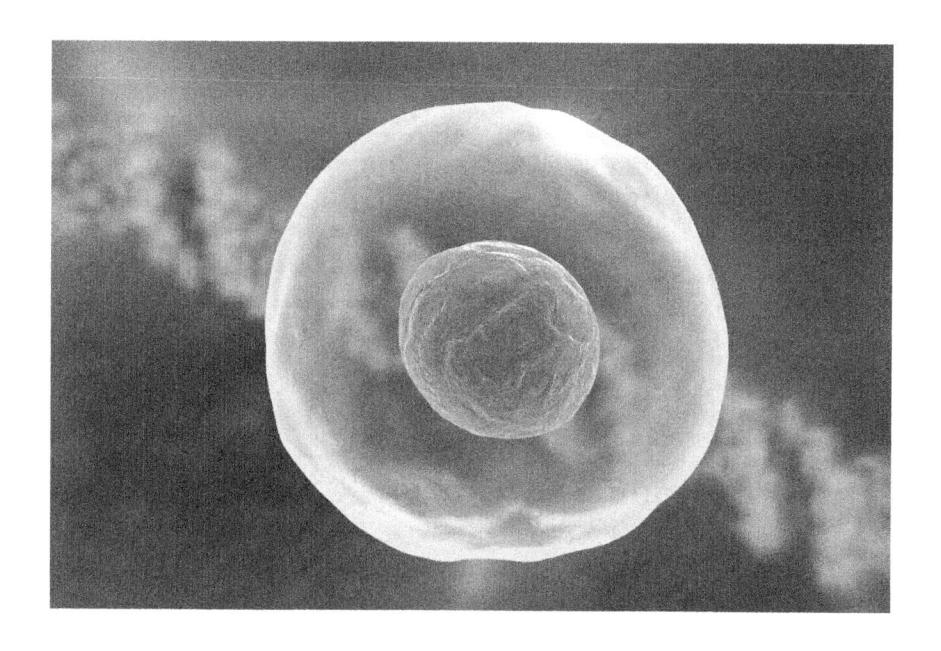

Objectives and Description

The Thought-Balloon Exercise deals with thoughts and beliefs that are on the surface – the ones you can easily detect when you are listening to the ticker tape of the thoughts running through your head. However, sometimes your surface beliefs don't fully explain your actions or behaviors. When this happens, you are most likely dealing with *nucleus beliefs* or core beliefs, those deeply rooted beliefs of how you view yourself, others, the future, and the world.

Just like a nucleus is the center core of an atom, nucleus beliefs are your center core of thinking. These beliefs are general rules in your thinking that are pervasive and experience-based, and they impact your resilience. Resilient thinking is strongly related to positive core beliefs.[25] Non-resilient thinking can be related to negative core beliefs that cause you to have out-of-proportion emotions and behaviors that arise at unexpected times.

Nucleus beliefs generally fall into three categories or themes that can be very common for residents and medical students[41]:
1. achievement
2. acceptance
3. control

Be Cautious of Stubborn Core Beliefs

Let's focus on the achievement category. Think about all you went through to get to where you are today. You had to do well in high school to get into college. You had to do well in college to get into medical school. You had to do well in medical school to get into residency. It's no wonder, then, that many residents and medical students have a nucleus belief related to achievement like, "Anything less than perfect is a failure."

Think about that core belief with the following scenario:

> You are on call and studying for an examination when a nurse pages three times. You get very angry and yell at the nurse. This is unlike you and your reaction doesn't really fit the situation.

Could your reaction be related to an underlying achievement nucleus belief?

The only way to address your nucleus beliefs is by uncovering them. Sometimes you can do this by asking yourself a series of "what" questions that are non-judgmental, trying to look deeper and deeper to get to your core underlying beliefs. That might go something like this:

- *What does it mean to you if the nurse keeps paging you?*
  "The nurse keeps paging me for unnecessary things and does not respect my time."

- *What is the most upsetting part of that for you?*
  "If the nurse keeps paging me, then I won't be able to study for my examination."

- *What is the worst part of that for you?*
  "If I can't study for my examination, I am not going to do well on it."

- *What does that say about you?*
  "Doing poorly means I will not be considered a good resident/medical student by the faculty."

- *What is so bad about that?*
  "I believe that anything less than perfect is a failure."

Finally, you get to that underlying core belief that led to the initial out-of-character, extreme response.

Nucleus Beliefs Exercise Instructions

Now that you have seen an example, it is your turn to try the Nucleus Beliefs Exercise. Monitor behaviors and actions that are out of character for you or are unnecessarily extreme. In these circumstances, try going down the "what" trail and fill out the worksheet below (or create your own version in your favorite electronic format). You can change the order of the "what" questions if it helps you get to your nucleus belief.

Nucleus Beliefs Worksheet

What concerning behavior or action is out of character for you or out of proportion to the situation?	
"What" Questions	
What does that mean to you?	
What is the most upsetting part of that for you?	
What is the worst part of that for you?	
What does that say about you?	
What is so bad about that?	

Other Interventions

Many people find that the deep-rooted, underlying beliefs are the most difficult to address. But once they are on the surface, you can deal with them. If you are having difficulty bringing your nucleus beliefs to the surface or dealing with them once they are on the surface, you may want to consider going beyond the resources available in these resilience exercises. Nucleus beliefs need to be properly addressed, because negative core beliefs can sometimes be linked to traumatic stress from childhood or other negative life experiences.

Sometimes residency-based or medical-school wellness programs conducted in a facilitated, trusting workshop environment may be helpful in building your resilience. Many such group-based interventions, however, may not delve into childhood memories and coping styles for all participants.[24] A personalized, one-on-one therapeutic relationship could be a more appropriate, effective, and evidenced-based setting for addressing deeply rooted core beliefs that are, for some, factors related to or contributing to depression, anxiety disorders, and other mental health problems.

Therapeutic relationships should not just focus on the negative. They should also access persistent, positive views about your trustworthiness, lovability, and the value of close relationships, all of which are key to resilience building.[42,43]

CHAPTER 11
GAUSSIAN THOUGHT-DISTRIBUTION EXERCISE

How wonderful it is that nobody need wait a single moment before starting to improve the world.

Ann Frank

Objectives and Description

This Gaussian Thought-distribution exercise teaches you how to use the best evidence on hand to put things into perspective. This exercise will help you stay focused and improve the accuracy of your thinking. You will learn to use probability distribution to determine the likelihood of an event actually occurring, which will result in a reduction in anxiety and build resilience.[44]

As a clinician, you are already used to applying science to the care of your patients. You use practice guidelines based on the best scientific evidence available at the present time; based on scientific data, you can create Gaussian distribution curves to help you determine which medication is most likely to help a patient with a specific condition or disease.

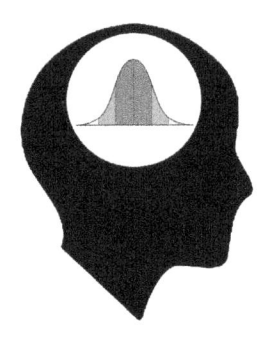

Similarly, this exercise teaches you how to use science to change your thinking to be more accurate. Through this simple exercise you can determine the probability distribution of an event actually occurring. Using science, you can reduce anxiety and build your resilience.

Driving Anxiety

By now you are probably pretty in tune with your thinking styles and patterns. Let's go back and revisit your B-to-C connections from Chapter 3, "Resilience." There, you began to determine whether you have any strong and consistent connections:

- Do you experience any feelings or emotions more than others?
- Do you tend to feel angry, sad, guilty, anxious, or embarrassed?

Take a minute to review those important B-to-C connections.

C (Feelings or Emotions)	B (Thoughts or Beliefs)
Anger	You perceive that your rights have been violated in some way.
Sadness or depression	You are sensing a loss of self-worth or that there is a real-word loss.
Guilt	You think that you have violated someone else's rights.
Anxiety or fearfulness	You perceive some type of threat in the future.
Embarrassment	You are negatively comparing yourself to others.

What did you determine was your go-to feeling or emotion? If you have a tendency to perceive some type of threat in the future, one that causes anxiety or fearfulness, this Gaussian Thought-Distribution Exercise is for you.

Let's look how this B-to-C connection can play out in residency:

Marty, a first-year resident, was one of the top candidates for his residency program. He went to a very prestigious college and medical school and has always performed in the top five percent of his class and on standardized tests. He recently started a new rotation and is on his second night of call. He prides himself on writing very complete and high-quality patient notes. He just admitted three new patients and ran them by his senior resident, who agreed with Marty's management plan.

Finally, at 3:30 a.m., Marty gets to the call room. He has trouble falling asleep, and after just a few minutes of sleep he wakes up in a panic. He thinks he might have forgotten to write an order on a patient. He mumbles to himself, "How could I have done that? The nurse is probably going to find out I forgot to place an order on my patient. The nurse is going to call my senior resident and complain. My senior resident is going to contact the residency program director and tell him I am incompetent. The residency program director is going to tell the chairperson of the department that I am not fit to be a resident in this hospital and I will get fired, and then I will never be able to find another job in medicine, I won't be able to pay my rent, and I will lose everything including my girlfriend."

This line of thinking is called *catastrophizing*. Catastrophizing happens when we imagine the worst possible outcome of an action or event. It is cognitive distortion that makes a situation into a catastrophe when it is not. Although many of us will occasionally awaken in the middle of the night worried we have forgotten something, individuals who are prone to anxiety often experience catastrophic thinking. They regularly focus on what can go wrong in the future. Although Marty's catastrophic thinking may seem a bit ridiculous to an objective observer, it certainly feels real and accurate to him in the moment.

Gaussian Distribution of the Mind Exercise Instructions

Let's take a scientific approach to see if we can help Marty put things into perspective.

Step 1: Thought Deconstruction

In medicine, it is common to do task deconstructions to break down any procedure into its component parts. By doing this, it is easier to teach how to recognize, avoid, and mange any errors or complications that might occur at each step of a procedure. The Gaussian Thought Distribution Exercise takes the same approach.

The first step is to do a thought deconstruction. List each thought separately, so you can record it as it occurred and can analyze it individually. That way you can avoid, recognize, and manage any distorted thoughts you might have.

Marty's thoughts can be broken down into eight parts:

Thought Deconstruction
1. I forgot to write an order on my patient.
2. The nurse is going to find out I forgot to write the order.
3. The nurse is going to call my senior resident and complain.
4. My senior resident is going to contact the residency program director and tell him I am incompetent.
5. The chairperson will fire me.
6. I will never be able to find another job in medicine.
7. I won't be able to pay my rent.
8. I will lose everything including my girlfriend.

Step 2: Anchoring With a Best Case Scenario

After the thought deconstruction exercise, you can clearly see that some of the thoughts are absurd and extremely unlikely. Daniel Kahneman, a famous experimental psychologist who won the Nobel Prize, worked with Amos Tversky to understand cognitive bias. They conducted experiments demonstrating that if your thinking is skewed in a particular direction, it influences the choices you make.[45] This is known as the *anchoring effect*.

The following example that illustrates their work. If you are asked the question, "Was Hippocrates over 40 years old when he died?" you may respond that he was 50 or 60 years old. If you are asked a similar question, but with a different anchoring value, "Was Hippocrates over 100 years old when he died?" you may respond that he was 80 or 90 years old.

The age of Hippocrates' death, of course, did not change—he was 90 years old when he died—but the anchoring effect influenced your thought process.

The same is true with feelings and emotions. If you have a tendency to be anxious, your thinking is going to be skewed to the anchor of perceiving that there is likely to be some type of threat in the future.

You need to change your anchor. You can do that with a simple exercise called *anchoring with a best-case scenario*. As part of this exercise, you are going to help Marty create a possible best-case scenario that is just as absurd as his worst-case scenario. It might go something like this:

> Finally, at 3:30 a.m., Marty gets to the call room. He has trouble falling asleep and after a few minutes of sleep he wakes up in a panic. He thinks he might have forgotten to write an order on a patient.
>
> He says to himself, "I better run out and add the order as quickly as I can." He hurries to the nursing station, puts the order into the EHR, and tells the nurse that he made the change. The nurse is so impressed with Marty's dedication, honesty, and integrity that she sends an email to the residency program director. The program director is so moved by the email that he tells the chairperson. In honor of the event, the chairperson creates new award called the "Resident Dedication Award." He lets Marty know that he will be the first recipient of the award and that he is going to double Marty's salary, stating that he is now a role model for all of the other residents. Marty later lists the award on his CV, and that is the reason he gets into a top fellowship in the subspecialty of his choice. His girlfriend decides that since he was recognized for his dedication, honesty, and integrity that she wants to marry him. They get married four months later and live happily ever after.

Equally as absurd, the new best-case scenario anchor will help Marty improve the accuracy of his thinking and fight his cognitive distortion. With these new anchors, let's go back to Marty's original thoughts and estimate the likelihood that they will occur.

Thought Deconstruction	Likelihood
1. I forgot to write an order on my patient.	90%
2. The nurse is going to find out I forgot to write the order.	75%
3. The nurse is going to call my senior resident and complain.	10%
4. My senior resident is going to contact the residency program director and tell him I am incompetent.	1 in a thousand
5. The chairperson will fire me.	1 in a million
6. I will never be able to find another job in medicine.	1 in 2 million
7. I won't be able to pay my rent.	1 in 3 million
8. I will lose everything including my girlfriend.	1 in 3 million

Step 3: Create a Gaussian Distribution Curve

Before the anchoring exercise, Marty may have only considered the left half of the Gaussian curve, reflecting his tendency toward anxiety and the worst-case scenarios.

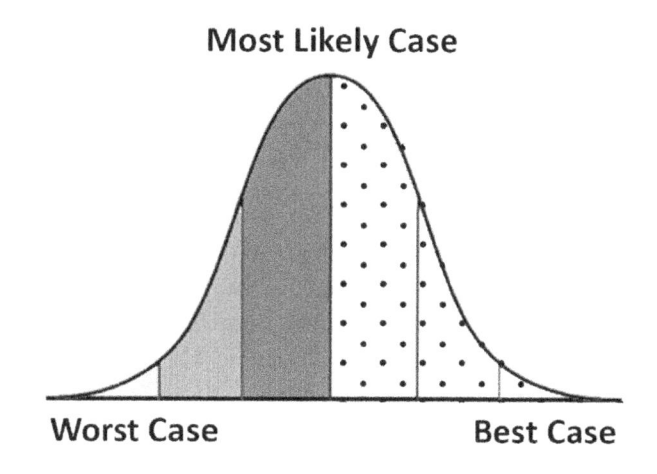

Most Likely Case

Worst Case   **Best Case**

But following the anchoring exercise, Marty may be more inclined to consider the full curve and focus in on the most likely scenarios in the Gaussian distribution, which will more accurately reflect realistic thinking.

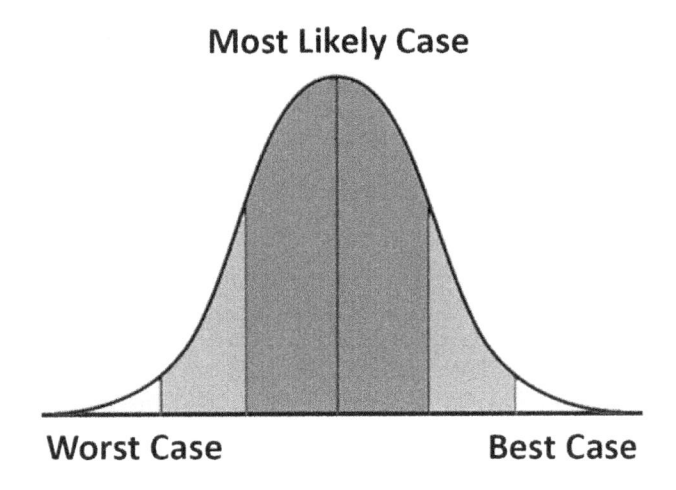

Most Likely Case

Worst Case **Best Case**

Step 4: Likely Outcomes and Solutions

The final step of the process is to outline the most likely outcome and potential solutions. This not only helps you think more accurately, but also helps you be proactive and get into problem-solving mode.

The likely outcomes would include:
- Immediately put the order into the EHR.
- Call the nurse right away to make sure she knows about the missed order.
- Since it has been less than an hour since Marty missed putting in the order, round on the patient to make sure there is no change in status.
- Learn from the experience and create process improvements for the department. Develop an order sheet or checklist for patients with similar problems since one does not already exist. Review order sheets/checklists that exist for other problems. See if there are any other gaps that need to be filled.

Gaussian Thought-Distribution Worksheet

Use the following worksheet for future Gaussian Thought-Distribution Curve Exercises.

Worst-Case Thought Deconstruction	Likelihood	Best-Case Thought Deconstruction	Likely Outcomes and Solutions
1.			
2.			
3.			
4.			
5.			
6.			
7.			
8.			
9.			
10.			
11.			
12.			

CHAPTER 12
NARRATIVE MEDICINE EXERCISE

Confront the dark parts of yourself, and work to
banish them with illumination and forgiveness.
Your willingness to wrestle with your demons will
cause your angels to sing.

August Wilson, American Playwright

Objectives and Description

This exercise teaches the concept of narrative medicine and describes three simple steps for participating in this resilience exercise, focused on reflecting and sharing, nurturing empathy, and compassion. It may seem counterintuitive that teaching humaneness is necessary, but the real outcome of the Narrative Medicine Exercise is not how to care, but how to *keep* caring while fostering resilience.[46]

Let's consider some of the realities of medical school, residency, and the practice of medicine. Doctors are expected to tap into their own sense of empathy to deliver effective patient care. At the same time, professionalism requires the preservation of boundaries whereby the health provider's emotions are necessarily compartmentalized, lest busy doctors let down their guard. A senior resident or medical student may admit a familiar continuity patient who dies hours after admission. An intern could be post-call following a night managing multiple trauma victims, several of whom don't make it.

The Narrative Medicine Exercise is a powerful tool to promote reflection, processing, and sharing the challenges of this very demanding work.

Reflecting and Sharing

Emotional Reserve and Objectivity

Emotional reserve and objectivity are not only challenged in the face of tragic outcomes in medicine, but are also necessary when addressing angry patients, when broaching topics outside a provider's comfort zone, and when handling the multiple demands of the day. For example, death certificates still need to be signed;

the next patient is awaiting admission; and the critically ill need to be presented the following morning. Grief, guilt, and other feelings must be put on hold to perform one's duties on the wards or in the clinic.

The Narrative Medicine Exercise provides a safe space for reflection and sharing as a means to process emotions following challenging clinical experiences.[47]

Stories Have the Power to Heal

The premise of the Narrative Medicine Exercise is that stories have the power to heal. Telling your story is as important as listening to the stories of colleagues. Through active reflection—which could involve journaling, essaying or poetry—you can gain personal insight into the meaning of illness and the limitations of being a healer while celebrating the triumphs of the human spirit.

The success of this exercise is based on your willingness to personally write, reflect, and then share your thoughts and beliefs with your colleagues. When sharing in a group setting it is imperative to create an environment of trust, non-judgment, and active participation by all.

A narrative medicine exercise group-activity may begin by broaching a topic, offering the chance to read a short passage, and then allowing time for participants to set down their thoughts in writing. A sharing session follows, which could involve each person reading what he or she just wrote, followed by a facilitated time for colleagues to provide supportive feedback.[46] It is best if participants are given protected time for this exercise by the department or program so that clinical responsibilities are not a distraction.

Narrative Medicine Exercise Instructions

There are three steps to the Narrative Medicine Exercise: reading, writing, and sharing.

Step 1: Read

Read passages as a group on a thematic topic area. Potential group activity topics paired with examples of publications that can be used for readings are shown below.[46,48]

- **Death and Dying**: *Physicians' Reflections*[49] and *The Initiation*[50]
- **Pregnancy Loss**: *Nesting in a Season of Light*[51]
- **Cultural Competency**: *War Dances*[52]
- **Domestic Violence and Sexual Abuse**: *Power*[53]
- **Work-life Balance**: *Bullet in the Brain*[54]
- **Caring for the Underserved**: *55-Word Stories*[55]
- **Self-care**: *How Do Young Doctors Find Balance After a 28-hour Workday?*[56]
- **Becoming a Doctor**: *She Makes the First Cut*[57]
- **Coping with Tragedy**: *The Absolute Worst Thing*[58]
- **The Fallible Doctor**: *Making Mistakes*[59]
- **The Doctor-Patient Relationship**: *The Art of Medicine*[60]

Find out if your department or institution offers specific reading materials as a part of this Narrative Medicine Exercise.

Step 2: Write

It is healing to write about your own experiences with patients, their families, and your healthcare colleagues. Creative pieces—including poetry and even brief, scripted scenes that are acted out—could be part of the sharing component of a narrative medicine session. Or you may simply write a paragraph reflecting on a passage you've just read, with self-references to clinical experiences and self-reflection or reactions to them.

You might want to increase your writing activities to daily journaling. Journaling can be a significant stress-reliever and is a powerful outlet to process raw, fresh experiences. It can also be used as a method to process emotional responses that need to be postponed and temporarily controlled as part of impulse regulation, which is another essential resilience trait.

Reading Reflection
To get you started on Narrative Medicine Exercise, below is a real-life experience from one of this book's authors.[60]

The Art of Medicine

About 25 years ago, very early in my career, I was on call and covering the emergency room for the Ob/Gyn department. During my shift, a hospital administrator that I knew came into the ED feeling sick and experiencing a sudden high fever. She was dizzy, feeling faint, and rapidly becoming confused. She had a strange bright red rash on her body.

First, she was evaluated by the emergency medicine physicians, who then called the infectious disease consultants, and finally by the surgeons. Her condition was deteriorating rapidly but none of them could figure out what was going on with her, so they called me in to take a look. Immediately, I knew she had a very rare condition called Toxic Shock Syndrome. I had never seen a person with this condition before, but I knew the condition had a very high mortality rate and we had to act quickly. We began very aggressive medical treatment and transferred her to the intensive care unit. Even with all of our best efforts, she became extremely hypotensive, was intubated and placed on a respirator, and finally went into a deep coma.

Everyone was sure she was going to die and that she had an irreversible brain injury. Everyone except for me, that is. My conclusion was not based on any science. I don't know why to this day, but I had this gut feeling that she could and would recover. That was my mindset every day during my rounds. I would close the door to her room and privately talk to her. I would update her on her condition and tell her that I was hopeful she would get better and continue to play the important role in the hospital that she had before her illness. I would hold her hand and tell her how much the hospital needed her. I did this every day for a month without a response.

Then one day, when I held her lifeless hand during my rounds, her finger twitched. It was extremely subtle, but it was enough to get my heart racing. I sat there with great anticipation waiting for another movement to convince myself that I didn't image it. When the second twitch came a few seconds later, I jumped up and sprinted out of the room to find the nursing staff so they could witness this "miracle." A parade of onlookers jammed into the room in disbelief. There was complete silence in the room as they watched and waited. Then her foot twitched. Cheers and applause erupted in the room, like you might hear when someone from your country wins an Olympic gold medal.

The anticipation grew the next day when there was even more movement…and the next…and the next, until finally she opened her eyes. Everyone thought it was a miracle, especially when we realized that she could clearly understand everything we were saying. Her brain function seemed completely intact.

She dramatically improved over the next several days. When she was finally extubated, she began talking for the first time in over a month. The first words that she said were, "Dr. Levy, I heard everything that you said to me over the last month, and that is what kept me alive." We both sat there in silence and cried.

From that day forward, I was a true believer in the "art of medicine" and that healing is much more than prescribing medication and performing surgery. This experience changed the way I viewed and practiced medicine. It didn't take me long to start my journey to try to understand the mind-body connection, and how mental and emotional conditions can influence medical outcomes.

I continued my Ob/Gyn medical practice with vigor and hope. I also started working with experts in wellness, positive psychology, burnout, anxiety, depression, and resilience to expand my thinking and to improve the efficacy of the care I provided to my patients.

- Jeffrey Levy, MD

Please reflect on your thoughts and feelings about this passage. Does it relate to any experiences you have had with patients? Do you believe in the "art of medicine"?

Use the space below to capture your thoughts and reactions, or type them into your computer or mobile device.

Original Narrative Writing

Some people have difficulty writing about something they have read and would prefer to write an original narrative from their own experiences. If this helps, you may want to try writing about themes like something that was new to you, something that surprised you, something that deeply moved you, or something that made you feel good. Try to write it under 15 minutes. It does not have to be perfect and polished. The goal is to share something important and meaningful to you with your colleagues.

Below is an example of an original narrative writing piece by one of the authors regarding a new experience for him.

> I traveled 20 hours not knowing what to expect. It was my first time in this part of the world. I didn't know the culture. I didn't know their education and knowledge level. I didn't even know how well they would understand me.
>
> I had been invited to Ethiopia by the American College of Obstetricians and Gynecologists and the Ethiopian Ministry of Health to teach healthcare providers about curriculum development and e-learning. I was asked to develop and conduct a 36-hour seminar over four days. The task was a bit daunting, but one that excited me. I felt up to the challenge.
>
> The first day of the course, one of the participants—an Ob/Gyn—arrived to the program an hour late and was very apologetic. I later found out that she had been dealing with a maternal and fetal mortality all night. A patient in the Ethiopian public health system had been laboring for several days at home but could not get to a hospital. She was finally taken to the hospital after she ruptured her uterus and her baby was expelled into the abdominal cavity. Both mother and baby died on the way to the hospital. After going through what I considered to be an extraordinarily traumatic situation, the physician was a bit tired, but she was poised and ready to learn. After all, this was <u>not</u> an uncommon occurrence there; the maternal mortality rate in some sub-Saharan African

countries is the highest in the world at approximately 1 in 74 mothers giving birth.

Think about that – 1 in 74 women die in childbirth! This is incomprehensible for some "high resource" countries with the lowest maternal mortality rates of about 1 in 33,000. How can we allow this disparity? This is one of the main reasons that I went to Ethiopia: to share some knowledge and skills with healthcare providers to help reduce the maternal mortality rate across the country, and possibly even one day throughout the continent.

The first day of the seminar was going extremely well. The participants were engaged, intelligent, and had a surprising grasp of technology – at least surprising to me. As I got to know the healthcare providers in the group, I realized how beautiful they were in spirit and character. I began to realize that they were the most resilient people I had ever met. That realization would be confirmed the next day.

Mid-afternoon on the second day of the course, we took a 15-minute break. We all congregated in a foyer in the hotel for coffee and tea and were having deep discussions about the educational needs for healthcare providers in Ethiopia. We were in one of the nicest hotels in Ethiopia and you could look up to the overcast sky through a glass roof over 20 stories above. Unbeknownst to us, there were some workers on the roof doing repairs that day.

We all heard it at the same time: what sounded like sonic boom coming from above. As we looked up toward the noise, we saw large chunks of concrete and glass shrapnel from the roof barreling down toward our group. Everyone scattered out of instinct to get out of the way. Some of the course participants were hit by pieces of glass and injured. We immediately went from student/teacher mode to healthcare provider mode. We triaged the injuries and sent three people to the local hospital.

We quickly found out that there was a worker accident on the roof that caused the collapse of a small section. When I surveyed the foyer area after the situation was under control, I realized that the table where I was drinking coffee and sharing insights during the break had been cut in half by a large chunk of concrete. I took a picture of the table that had been destroyed and thought to myself, "What if…"

We decided to take the rest of the day off from the conference, but we wanted to be together and process what we had just experienced. We moved to another area of the hotel and sat in a circle talking about the people who were injured and wondering how they were doing. We told stories of some of the worst things that have happened to us in our lives, and that seemed to be somewhat calming for the group. As we shared stories, our comradery continued to grow. We had just been together in a near death experience and we formed a bond closer than I could have imagined. We were from different cultures, different countries, almost different worlds. But in the end, we were all caring human beings who had gone through the same traumatic experience.

The next day we came back to the course with renewed vigor, enthusiasm, and cohesiveness. We were heartened to hear that the injured participants were released from the hospital. They came back to the course with bandages covering different parts of their bodies, but participated fully as if nothing had ever happened. We finished the day talking about how grateful we were to have shared our time and experiences with one another.

After the course, I spent a day exploring Addis Ababa, the capital of Ethiopia. I immersed myself as much as possible into the culture. I was emotionally distraught by the extreme poverty I observed, but at the same time I seemed to absorb the incredible strength and dignity the people carried in the midst of their adversity.

I truly believe I am a better person following my trip to Ethiopia. I am already looking forward to going back there again soon.

-Jeffrey Levy, MD

Step 3: Share

Remember that to be successful in this exercise, your department/school must create a safe environment of trust and non-judgment for you to share personal insights and feelings. The success of this process may also be improved if faculty members participate who are familiar with the Narrative Medicine Exercise and who are trained facilitators.

In your first session, share your writings about the story of the patient in the coma or your original narrative writing with your colleagues. It is most powerful if you read your writings out loud to the group. Provide positive feedback to one another regarding how what others wrote impacted you. If you are more comfortable, you can share your feedback anonymously on small pieces of paper. Then you will have taken the first step of the Narrative Medicine Exercise!

At the end of each session, discuss what worked well and what components could be improved. Then begin to read about other topics regarding humane and compassionate care of patients. It is best if each session has its own theme so that everyone can focus on one topic area. In a short period of time, it will become easier for you to share your writings with other residents and medical students, and for them to share theirs with you.

Continue the process of writing, reflecting, and sharing narratives that nourish the empathetic doctor-patient relationship. If done on a regular basis, this exercise can positively impact your medical philosophies and practices. Plan to consider how this Narrative Medicine Exercise impacts your compassion and empathy on a regular basis.

CHAPTER 13
PERSONAL MISSION STATEMENT EXERCISE

A personal mission statement becomes the DNA
for every other decision we make.

Stephen Covey, Author

Objectives and Description

Learn to craft a mission statement describing your overall purpose for going into medicine as well as the meaning in day-to-day life as a doctor-in-training. With difficulties and challenges typical of medical school and residency, everyday hurdles may make you feel like you are deep-sea diving through murky waters, having to come up for air every so often. You have worked hard, made a difference in the lives of patients and families, and set an example of professionalism to colleagues, but the mud and seaweed kicked up from daily life on the wards or in clinic could obscure the beautiful coral reef just inches away.

A carefully crafted mission statement will help you to put your medical training experience in perspective and to keep front-and-center the sustained vision of your long-term goal while acknowledging the potential to grow with daily challenges. Maintaining a positive perspective is an essential aspect of resilience—a stable, optimistic point of view helps you look forward to your professional development. That kind of optimism will be captured in your mission statement.[61,62]

The Importance of a Mission Statement

Maintaining Perspective

To maintain perspective, read, memorize, and recite your mission statement. Call to mind your mission statement and you will see the coral reef come into view again. You will be grounded in the realization that the individual patients you round on daily are human beings you treat, while marveling at each patient's humanity and diversity. Each patient can be a source of wonder, like the multi-colored organisms that make up the fragile beauty of a coral reef.

Your mission statement will also help you to snorkel above on the surface to marvel at the overall, massive, interactive ecosystem of this coral reef, representing the larger *why* in your "why I became a doctor" statement.

Microscope and Telescope

The mission statement serves both as a microscope and a telescope. It is a microscope in the sense that your mission statement has a perspective on your short-term goals—the here and now. It is like seeing the tiny, colorful organisms in the coral reef that reflect your heartfelt values, such as compassion, search for knowledge, and meaning in life that enable you to make your training environment a place that nurtures those values.

It is a telescope in the sense that your mission statement also houses your long-term, more distant objectives regarding why you became a doctor. These are the words that rekindle your long-term perspective, clearing the haze so you see the big picture, drawing it closer to you in order to avoid making negative predictions about your future based on current adversities.

Finding Commonality

Resilience workshops could include an activity for composing your own mission statement as part of a group activity in a supportive setting, one that validates your unique values and experiences. Sharing with the group allows for a collective point of view to highlight shared values, which may augment or help modify and fine-tune the final product. Residents and medical students can find common elements with peers—shared experiences and perspectives—that can be interwoven with an individual mission statement. The end result is all the more compelling and conducive to resilience.

During your resilience workshops, if not already part of the curriculum, suggest that the group work together on crafting a mission statement. Residents and medical students who have completed this exercise find both satisfaction and validation through the process of creating this statement when crafted in a trusting, confidential small-group setting of peers.[34]

Medical and Personal Goals

Your mission statement should describe both your long-term objective for a career in medicine and your personal values and goals. It should answer not only "What kind of doctor do I want to become?" but also elucidate "What kind of person am I?"

The goal of sharing a mission statement is not to pressure you into writing yours one way or another, but to help validate what you have already written and open yourself up to new ways of expressing a shared vision with common values, a form of peer support essential both to professional fulfillment and resilience. The resulting mission statement is your own. It reflects your uniqueness and is capable of renewing your commitment to medicine. Like you, your personal statement is resilient, dynamic, and subject to change with new experiences.[34,61]

Personal Mission Statement Exercise Instructions

The Personal Mission Statement Exercise may include the following steps:

Step 1: Record Core Values

Core values are attributes or strong beliefs that serve as a roadmap for your code of conduct. There are a number of ways you can write down core values.

You may choose to write them as one-word adjectives like resourceful, compassionate, curious, and diligent. However, a single word may not be as valuable to you as an actionable sentence.

You can write simple declarative sentences as a means of best expressing core values. The sentences serve as guideposts for decision-making and help determine appropriateness of actions. These sentences could act as your collective microscope, helping you to see more clearly through the hardships of residency or medical school.

Here are some examples of core value sentences for daily living as a doctor-in-training[63]:

- I treat patients with my heart and mind (holistic care).
- Lifelong learning is a goal and daily source of joy (curiosity).
- I take pride when I help junior residents and peers master skills (teaching).
- A patient I cannot cure can teach me about living (dignity, compassion).

Step 2: Identify Your Success Vision

Answer the question, "What is my vision of success in medicine?" This statement within the statement is the view at the end of your telescope, helping you to see the larger goal of professional practice. The success vision, like your core values, is a mindset you carry around to help maintain an optimistic perspective with a long-term

goal. That success statement could reflect the kind of population you seek to treat or the specialty you aim to enter after residency. Example success sentences might be:
- I see myself practicing medicine while striving for competence and personal well-being.
- I see myself practicing medicine in a community where I see making positive change.
- I see myself practicing medicine in a setting where I can use my hands to heal.

An example of a mission statement from one of the authors is provided below.

> My mission is to apply my curiosity, compassion, empathy, love of learning, and persistence to heal and build a better world. My vision of success is to collaborate with top healthcare providers in every field and impart their knowledge so others can deliver the highest quality, evidence-based care to positively impact the lives of millions of patients on a global scale.
>
> -Jeffrey Levy, MD

Write your mission statement in the space provided on the next page or in an electronic format on your preferred device.

Step 3: Learn From Your Peers

A group session that includes crafting and sharing a mission statement gives you an opportunity to gain insight into how similar your values and goals are to those of your peers. Listen for those similarities, but be mindful of your uniqueness. Revise your statement accordingly.

Step 4: Test Your Mission Statement

As you go through rotations, you may find the content of your mission statement is challenged in a good way. Remember that your mission statement is dynamic. Build upon new experiences by asking yourself if what you learned and witnessed can augment and grow your mission statement.

CHAPTER 14
CRASH CART RESILIENCE EXERCISE

When fear rushed in, I learned how to hear my heart
racing but refused to allow my feelings to sway me.
That resilience came from my family.
It flowed through our bloodline.

Coretta Scott King

Objectives and Description

The exercises in this chapter are intended to help you relax in the moment. They provide you with "crash cart" tools that are focused on breathwork and visualization, and which can be used in real time when you are confronted with stressors. These exercises are intended for practice during dedicated time *before* you implement them in real-time. All you need to do is breathe and imagine.

Diaphragmatic breathing and *progressive muscle relaxation* are two mind-body methods for integrating intention and focus (cognition, power of the conscious mind) with somatic, autonomic (body) processes that elicit a relaxation response.[64] These and similar exercises can help you cope with stress by staying calm during challenging moments. The key word here is *moments*. Why? It takes only a few moments for powerful emotions to pass. These relaxation techniques can help you to work through the tough moments. Once you use your crash cart tools and find calm in chaos, you will have enhanced self-efficacy for handling adversity, a key component of resilience.

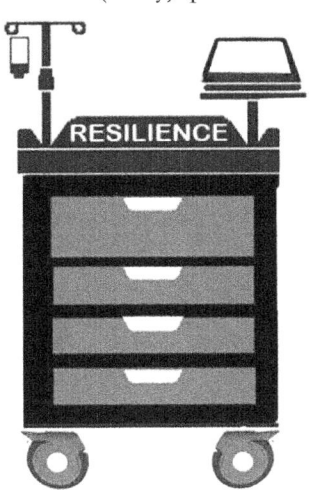

You will probably find parallels with what you are already practicing if your residency or medical school offers mind-body techniques for finding inner calm as part of its wellness curriculum. Training programs with a culture of wellness promote these types of techniques not only to foster resilience, but also to reduce stress and the risk of burnout.[24,34]

No matter where you go, you are breathing. Breathwork makes this exercise portable and readily available for a real-time relaxation response to stressors. However, rapid, shallow breathing is *not* the kind of air exchange conducive to relaxation; it is, rather, a common response to stress. If you find yourself breathing this way, use diaphragmatic (or abdominal) breathing techniques to become aware of your breathing and avoid the build-up of tension. With diaphragmatic breathing, you are consciously engaging in full respiratory excursion, helping to restore a sense of calm and relaxation.[24]

Diaphragmatic Breathing Instructions

Position
Sit in a quiet place on a comfortable chair with back support.

Hand Placement
Place one hand on your abdomen and one hand mid-chest.

Breathe and Be Mindful
Be aware of your breathing, attending to your inhalation and exhalation as well as the movement of your chest.

- **Inhalation**: Take a slow deep breath, noting the outward movement of your abdomen during inhalation. Picture your diaphragm contracting (flattening) as your lungs expand, or visualize an inflating balloon as you breathe in.
- **Exhalation**: Let the air out of your lungs with a slow, controlled, full exhalation while sensing the inward/downward displacement in the hand you've placed on your abdomen.
- **Chest Movement:** Be mindful of any motion of the hand on your chest. Is it moving? You should try to avoid chest motion during this exercise. Remember that shallow, rapid breathing is stress breathing, which concentrates movement in the chest as opposed to the relaxed, full-breaths initiated by the diaphragm during relaxed breathing.

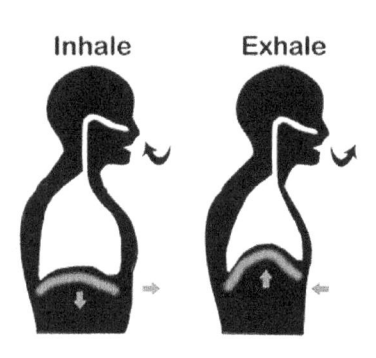

Duration
Take three seconds for each inhalation and exhalation. Repeat the cycle three times. Practice this exercise for about five minutes a day.

Progressive Muscle Relaxation

The autonomic nervous system unconsciously builds up muscle tension as part of multiple fight-flight responses throughout the day. Progressive muscle relaxation (PMR) is a stress-relieving technique for scanning your whole body and sensing where this tension has built up. Once you are proficient with the full-body PMR, the "fast-action-scan" crash cart application of PMR hones in on the stress-burdened muscle group, enabling you to focus on known tightness when encountering a stressor for a quick-acting relaxation response,[65] and to release tension before the somatic stress response escalates.

Tension-Relaxation Cycling

As part of this PMR exercise, you'll use a tension-relaxation cycle (TRC)—a flexion (tension)-extension (relaxation) couplet for muscle groups. For a given muscle or muscle group, while taking slow deep breaths, hold muscle tension for five seconds and then relax for 10-15 seconds. Keep all other areas relaxed when focusing on a TRC in one spot. Another TRC approach is to tense/relax limbs at the same time rather than individually.

Note that for some areas you need not actually move joints, but merely use an isometric contraction for the involved muscles while keeping the limb in place. For other muscle groups, actual limb movement is preferable.

How you employ the TRC for each area is up to you. For example, if you sense tension in your lower back following your scan, rather than tensing those muscles, engage in the relaxation-only phase of the TRC.

PMR Instructions

Position
Sit comfortably in a chair in a quiet place where you will not be distracted. Close your eyes.

Begin Scan
Take a few deep breaths and begin to mentally scan your body from head to toe, asking yourself, "Do I feel tight or tense anywhere in particular?" If you find a locus of tension, this is an area where you will either begin focusing the exercise or spend more time on relaxing any perceived tension.

Scan with TRCs
A suggested order is to scan from head to toe as follows:
- **Top of Head, Forehead, and Face**: Lift your eyebrows while furrowing your forehead (as you would when angry). At the same time, close your jaws (gently biting the upper and lower teeth together) while pressing the tip of your tongue to your palate and making your lips frown.
- **Neck and Shoulders**: Nod downward so your chin moves toward your chest while shrugging your shoulders.
- **Wrists and Forearms**: While bending your arm at the elbow, make a fist and flex your biceps, either one side at a time or both sides at once.
- **Chest**: Pull your shoulder blades back and toward each other as you tighten your chest and relax your arms by your sides.
- **Abdomen and Lower Back**: Tighten your abdomen as though bracing for a punch, while moving your upper back forward and toward your feet. You should feel tension in the lumbar area.
- **Leg**: Bend at the thigh while lifting your foot off the floor, and pull your upper leg inward toward you.
- **Calves and Feet:** Dorsiflex your ankles then plantar flex, followed by curling your toes up then downward.

Duration and Frequency

Practice for 10-15 minutes once per day, or as often as recommended in your program or school's wellness initiative.

CHAPTER 15
MANAGING CONFLICTS EXERCISE

> The most important thing in communication is hearing what isn't being said. The art of reading between the lines is a life-long quest of the wise.
>
> *Shannon L. Alder, Author*

Objectives and Description

This exercise teaches you how to diffuse anger as a first step toward conflict resolution. Confrontation is a reality in healthcare. Whether it is between doctor and patient, attending and resident or medical student, or arising from differences of opinion or perspective, confrontation could lead to angry exchanges that can be avoided. Once tempers are calm, the work of negotiation and problem solving can begin.

Conflict and underlying anger occur in clinical practice in a number of circumstances, such as when delivering bad news or upon disclosure of medical errors. Patients can react with harsh, accusatory words, even toward the most well-meaning healthcare providers. Among colleagues or between junior and senior staff, power clashes may emerge; in the face of displaced anger, such clashes could cascade into overt lapses in professional behavior.

To be angry is human, but to lose one's temper is a choice. You have the means to tap into your calm, reasoning self and resume the work of healing or learning—even when angry or fearful in the face of confrontation. Finding the negotiator and peacekeeper within you requires emotional regulation and effective communication, resilience-cultivating skills that preserve trusting bonds between doctor-patient or learner-teacher.[22,66]

This exercise helps you to find that place of calm in three steps:
 1. Know the angry monster.
 2. Resist first impulses.
 3. Communicate effectively.

Managing Conflict Exercise Instructions

This resilience-building exercise covers emotional regulation and effective communication in three steps.

Step 1: Know the Angry Monster

Make an Angry Face: There is no need to dissect, X-ray or conduct sophisticated tests. This is the angry monster within us all: just look in the mirror and make an angry face. Study your reflection and notice where anger lives on your face. Compare that image with what the angry face looks like on others.

Note the Sights: What did you see in the mirror? Did you see some of these common facial features?[66]
- hot, flushed cheeks
- eyebrows drawn closer
- furrowed forehead
- lips exposing teeth or closed tightly, ends downward, locked in a pouting frown

Feel the Anger: Sensations of anger, like the angry mask, are rooted in the primordial flight-or-fight response. The surge of catecholamines partially responsible for keeping our hunter-gatherer ancestors alive still flow from our adrenal glands. The heart pumps faster and stronger. With increased stroke volume, skeletal muscles contract, ready us to plunge against our enemy or run for life.

Know the Anger: Recognize that anger lives in your body as well as your face. Do you clench your fists? Sweat? Stand taller? Breathe faster? These are some of the first signs of the flight-or-fight response welling up inside you. Awareness of these signs can help you control your first impulses, before angry words start flying and you regret the moment they leave your lips. Anger self-awareness can also help avert physical violence.

Step 2: Resist First Impulses

Providing there is no physical threat, ignore the flight or fight response. Make a conscious decision to relax, breathe, and listen. Practice the relaxation and breathing techniques you learned in Chapter 14, "Crash Cart Resilience Exercise," but conduct it in an accelerated, rapid-sequence fashion:

Relax: Be aware of any tense muscles, noting that tension is different for everyone. Some people feel tightness in the face, lower back, or legs. Relax any tense muscles and be aware of the difference in sensation between tighter-tensed and looser-relaxed muscles. Practice your relaxed posture.

Breathe: Breath awareness is at the foundation of mindfulness and meditative wellness practice, including yoga and tai chi. Centering and focusing on your breathing is a quick way of relaxing. Take three or four slow, deep breaths, placing your awareness on your own breath cycle. Feel your belly expand upon inhalation and recede as you slowly exhale.

Listen: Be sure you are listening to the individual addressing you as you work on your own self-awareness.

Step 3: Communicate Effectively

Be aware of your body language and words.

Stand for Peace: You already accomplished the first step by taking a relaxed body stance. Maintain an open stance with your arms at your sides, or anywhere that will help you feel relaxed and most comfortable. You can put your hands in your pockets or clasp them gently by your belly. Avoid crossing your hands and arms across your chest because this is considered a confrontational posture.

Also avoid staring, but do look occasionally at the individual purposefully, with a sincere expression as though to say, "Yes, I understand," and "Yes, I hear you." In addition, move slowly and not suddenly.

Sound Like Peace: Use a calm, soft tone. Be aware of your voice's volume.

Speak for Peace: Acknowledge the person's grievance by repeating it back in your own words. Validate that you understand their frustration, irritation, or other feelings. Begin to offer solutions to the problem(s) or issue(s) the other person expressed. Monitor and listen for the response.

Listen for Peace: Give plenty of time for a response that may represent a de-escalation of the anger toward you.

Role-Playing Scenario

This is not an easy exercise for everyone. We all have a natural inclination to defend ourselves and to either fight back in words or recede and leave the situation. Sometimes it helps to pair up with another resident or student and role-play, or to work in a small group with a facilitator to practice conflict resolution and anger-diffusing skills.

For this exercise, pair up with another resident or medical student. One of you will play the physician and the other will be the patient in the following scenario:

> You have seen 12 patients in clinic and each had significant problems, so you are running way behind and have several more patients in the waiting room. You walk in to see your next patient and she is extremely angry. You notice several typical signs of anger including flushed cheeks, a furrowed forehead, and a pouting frown. You are barely in the examination room when she starts yelling at you.

Patient: "I have been waiting for so long! No one in this clinic cares about the patients."

Resident/Medical Student: Practice managing conflict.
- **Avoid your First Impulse**: Take an inventory of your body. Did you notice your body tense? Are there any areas of your body that are more affected than others? Take a few seconds to relax and breathe before you respond.
- **Stand for Peace**: Adopt a relaxing body stance.
- **Sound Like Peace**: Use a calm, soft tone.
- **Speak for Peace**: Acknowledge your patient's grievance by repeating it back in your own words and validate that you understand her frustration, irritation, or other feelings. Start to offer solutions to the problems or issues expressed.

Patient: Let the physician respond to you.

Resident/Medical Student:
- **Listen for Peace**: Give plenty of time for the patient's response, which may represent a de-escalation of her anger toward you.

Continue role-playing until you feel you have successfully managed the conflict. Then switch roles and practice the scenario again. Debrief with each other afterward to talk about what worked well and what could be changed to result in a better outcome.

CHAPTER 16
SELF-ASSESSMENT TOOLS

A true genius admits that he/she knows nothing.

Albert Einstein

Self-Assessment Categories

Throughout this book you have been exposed to different self-assessment tools that help you understand your starting points for wellness, resilience, and burnout. You have been determining your strengths and areas that you can work to improve.

In this chapter, all of the self-assessments you have already completed and several new ones are put in one place for your convenience. The hope is that you will continue to explore your perceptions and views of yourself, your world, and your future on a regular basis.

Five categories of tests are presented here, including:
1. happiness and wellness
2. resilience and optimism
3. burnout and depression
4. character strengths
5. meaning in life and work-life balance

Questionnaire Examples

Each category contains a few relevant questionnaires, descriptions regarding what each measures, and a website address to find each one. A total of 26 questionnaires are included. While most of them are free, you will have to pay for the few that are not publicly available.

Category	Measurement	Website
Happiness and Wellness		
Authentic Happiness Inventory	Measures overall happiness	https://www.authentichappiness.sas.upenn.edu/testcenter
WHO-5 scale	Measures well-being	https://www.psykiatri-regionh.dk/who-5/Pages/default.aspx

Subjective Happiness Scale	Assesses enduring happiness	http://sonjalyubomirsky.com/subjective-happiness-scale-shs/
Fordyce Emotions Questionnaire	Measures current happiness	https://www.authentichappiness.sas.upenn.edu/testcenter
Satisfaction with Life Scale	Measures life satisfaction	http://www.midss.org/content/satisfaction-life-scale-swl
Approaches to Happiness	Measures overall happiness	https://www.authentichappiness.sas.upenn.edu/testcenter
Well-Being Survey	Measures well-being	https://www.authentichappiness.sas.upenn.edu/testcenter
Resilience and Optimism		
Connor-Davidson resilience scale (CD-25)	Measures resilience strengths and vulnerabilities	http://www.connordavidson-resiliencescale.com/submit-ofr.php
Resilience Factor Inventory	Measures seven resilience factors	http://rfi.adaptivlearning.com/entry.aspx?id=a1s2d3
Optimism Test	Measures optimism about the future	http://www.optimi.org/test/testopen.htm
PERMA	Measures flourishing	https://www.authentichappiness.sas.upenn.edu/testcenter
Burnout and Depression		
Maslach Burnout Inventory (MBI)	Measures emotional exhaustion, depersonalization, and reduced personal accomplishments	https://www.mindgarden.com/314-mbi-human-services-survey
CES-D Questionnaire	Measures depression symptoms	http://www.chcr.brown.edu/pcoc/cesdscale.pdf
PANAS Questionnaire	Measures positive and negative affect	https://www.authentichappiness.sas.upenn.edu/testcenter

Category	Measurement	Website
Character Strengths		
VIA Survey of Character Strengths	Measures 24 character strengths	http://www.viacharacter.org
Gratitude Survey	Measures appreciation about the past	http://www.midss.org/content/gratitude-questionaire-gq-6
Grit Survey	Measures perseverance and passion	https://angeladuckworth.com/grit-scale/
Stress and Empathy Questionnaire	Measures empathy, stress, and overall health	https://www.authentichappiness.sas.upenn.edu/testcenter
Transgression Motivations Questionnaire	Measures forgiveness	http://www.midss.org/transgression-related-interpersonal-motivations-inventory-trim-18
Jefferson Scale of Physician Empathy	Measures the capacity to empathize with patients as a teachable skillset	https://www.jefferson.edu/university/skmc/research/research-medical-education/jefferson-scale-of-empathy.html
Meaning in Life and Work-Life Balance		
Meaning in Life Questionnaire	Measures meaningfulness	https://www.authentichappiness.sas.upenn.edu/testcenter
Close Relationships Questionnaire	Measures attachment style	https://curiosity.com/topics/take-the-close-relationships-questionnaire-to-measure-your-attachment-style-curiosity/
Compassionate Love Scale	Measures tendency to support, help, and understand other people	http://www.midss.org/content/companionate-love-scale

Work-Life Questionnaire	Measures work-life satisfaction	https://www.authentichappiness.sas.upenn.edu/testcenter
Postgraduate Hospital Education Environment Measure (PHEEM)	Measures attitudes toward the training environment	https://www.pmcv.com.au/education/pheem/victorian-pheemprogram
Professional Fulfillment Index (PFI)	Measures physicians' professional fulfillment and burnout	https://link.springer.com/article/10.1007%2Fs40596-017-0849-3

Getting Started

We suggest you explore all of the questionnaires because you will learn something about yourself from each of them. Most take 5-20 minutes to complete. You may want to start with these:

- Authentic Happiness Inventory
- Subjective Happiness Scale
- Satisfaction with Life Scale
- Connor-Davidson Resilience Scale (CD-25)
- Maslach Burnout Inventory
- CES-D Questionnaire
- VIA Survey of Character Strengths
- Grit Survey
- Work-Life Questionnaire
- Postgraduate Hospital Education Environment Measure

Burnout and wellness can change throughout your career and during difficult life situations. Consider doing these self-assessments on a regular basis so you can keep in tune with your thinking and your wellness needs.

You can also seek out other assessment tools for yourself. Don't be afraid to share them with your fellow medical students or residents as long as your department/institution creates a safe environment for you to do so.

The VIA Survey of Character Strengths

One of the longer but most interesting questionnaires is the VIA Survey of Character Strengths. It is a validated survey that assesses 24 character strengths—your positive traits or capacities that contribute to personal fulfillment and the virtues (human goodness) that bring benefit to others. Character strengths are important, because the literature shows that if you use your greatest character strengths on a regular basis, you will be happier and find life more fulfilling.[67]

The 24 character strengths outlined on viacharacter.org include:
1. creativity (originality, ingenuity)
2. curiosity (interest, novelty-seeking)
3. open-mindedness (judgment, critical thinking)
4. love of learning
5. perspective (wisdom)
6. bravery (valor)
7. persistence (perseverance, industriousness)
8. integrity (authenticity, honesty)
9. vitality (zest, enthusiasm, vigor, energy)
10. love
11. kindness (generosity, nurturance, caring)
12. social intelligence (emotional and personal intelligence)
13. citizenship (social responsibility, loyalty, teamwork)
14. fairness
15. leadership
16. forgiveness and mercy
17. humility/modesty
18. prudence
19. self-regulation (self-control)
20. appreciation of beauty and excellence (awe, wonder)
21. gratitude
22. hope (optimism, future-mindedness)
23. humor (playfulness)
24. spirituality (religiousness, faith, purpose)

Go through the VIA Survey and learn about your top five character strengths.

CHAPTER 17
WELLNESS PROGRAM EXAMPLES

We should never permit ourselves to do anything that we are not willing to see our children do. We should set them an example that we wish them to imitate.

Brigham Young

Sharing Common Objectives

The increasing number of residency-based wellness programs share common objectives, not only to prevent burnout, but also to improve trainee wellness and the quality of patient care. A review of several effective resident wellness programs highlights their common attributes[7,15]:

- Disparate multifaceted interventions are part of an integrated curriculum.
- Programming is part of an overall culture of wellness, which includes consistent faculty endorsement and dedicated time for participants to pursue wellness activities.
- The curriculum is customized to residency program needs.
- Quality-checked and dynamic programming allows for change and improvement.

Defining Domains of Well-Being

Wellness interventions in residency programs across the United States tend to focus on several well-being defining domains[3,5]:

- **Autonomy or a Sense of Control**: providing an environment that promotes self-regulation and acting in accordance with one's values.
- **Sense of Competence**: acknowledgment of accomplishments through direct observation along with self-assessment to enhance self-awareness of professional development.
- **Physical Needs**: easy access to healthy foods and opportunities/settings for regular exercise.
- **Emotional Health**: teaching how to tap into a relaxation response using mind-body techniques like guided breathing, meditation, yoga, or tai chi. Yoga, for example, combines poses with deep breathing to improve flexibility while promoting stress reduction.

- **Social Support**: dedicated learning time, including workshops to teach self-care habits and how to recognize BOS, along with recreational activities to foster community spirit.

Implemented Wellness Models

There are no established guidelines for wellness interventions in post-graduate medical education. Consequently, the following examples are not intended to be representative of what you should do to aspire to a state of well-being and resilience, or what wellness programing steps your training program should institute. Rather, these are wellness models that have been implemented in the context of a study protocol, with wide approval among participants and published results demonstrating efficacy. Training programs have looked to these kinds of examples to guide their own wellness programming.[14]

It is important to note that not only are trainees satisfied with wellness interventions, but the rate of burnout—as well as the risks of depression and anxiety—are reduced where there is a high level of participation.[68,69]

A Curriculum to Teach Humanism and Reduce Burnout

Humanism is a core competency for professionalism in the practice of medicine. However, the usual role-modeling of humanistic attributes may not adequately empower residents with skillsets to overcome training-related stressors that threaten to undermine compassion, integrity, caring, and other values that patients associate with humane health professionals.

Through a two-phase exploratory study, investigators sought to determine whether a formal curriculum could not only improve the didactics of humanism, but also decrease burnout and foster resilience among a cohort of obstetrics/gynecology and internal medicine residents. The first phase involved thematic analysis of self-reflective essays in which participants were asked to describe instances when humanistic behaviors were challenged. Prominent themes including work-life balance, compassion fatigue, and difficult patient-doctor communication served as a needs assessment for formulating a series of humanism workshops. Three didactic sessions and completion of follow-up questionnaires constituted phase two, during which participant feedback was compared to that of a control group.

Validated scores for burnout and compassion were measured at baseline and following course completion. There was a statistically significant difference in both burnout and compassion scores compared to the controls, indicating a lower risk of burnout and improved humanism skills in those who took the course.

The authors recommended further study of a humanism curriculum in other residency programs for its potential to address burnout and improve the quality of post-graduate education.[70]

Crowdsourced Wellness Initiatives Database

In advance of a national summit, emergency medicine residencies created an online community to engender trust and collaboration among trainees to fast-track residency program wellness initiatives. The group formed a "Wellness Think Tank," consisting of 142 residents among 100 emergency medicine programs in the United States and Canada.[71] The collective's initial review of wellness programming revealed that residency programs were often creating their own in-house wellness programming because they were unaware of curricula in use at other programs. This revelation prompted the creation of an online, crowdsourced database of wellness initiatives, which includes brief descriptions of interventions along with educator resources. The goal is to facilitate more efficient change efforts than individual, siloed groups of trainees or residency programs could do on their own.

The platform also features:
- an online form to enter confidential feedback about existing wellness activities that would identify what works and facilitate adaptation to changing needs
- a step-by-step, downloadable guide for developing wellness programming

At the time of this book's publication, the aliem.com database included 38 initiatives describing a variety of interventions addressing all wellness domains including physical/mental health, social relatedness (team-building activities and support groups), and positive feedback/mentoring. The database continues to grow, proving that social media can be a catalyst among trainee stakeholders toward establishing a wellness culture in emergency medicine.

Physical Activity Reduces Burnout Risk

Lack of exercise is correlated not only with cardiovascular disease, but with an increased risk for burnout and depression during residency. For this reason, regular exercise is a common element of many wellness strategies among residency training programs.

Researchers at the University of Minnesota - Hennepin County Medical Center sought to validate this relationship in a group of interns who volunteered to complete a one-time survey that combined the MBI with questions to ascertain exercise habits. 78 interns from two internal medicine residency programs completed the questionnaire during the fall, approximately three months after beginning their training. Analysis of the data indicated [72]:
- Exercise levels decreased upon starting residency.

- 41% of participants failed to achieve Department of Health and Human Services physical activity guidelines; 68% of the less-active group met criteria for burnout.
- Obstacles to regular physical activity included lack of time, fatigue, and lack of access to a nearby health club or fitness facility.

The study underscores the need for wellness programs not only to promote the benefits of continued exercise during training, but to implement steps to reduce perceived barriers to staying fit.

Wellness and Suicide Prevention

The Resident and Faculty Wellness Program (RFWP) at Oregon Health & Science University provides several interventions including individual psychotherapy and structured group sessions, with the dual objectives of well-being promotion and suicide prevention. A longitudinal study of this cross-specialty program (after more than 10 years of implementation) demonstrated a consistent increase in utilization among residents and fellows, from 5.2% to 24.7%. Faculty participation also increased steadily.[4]

The authors considered the program successful based on sustained utilization and a high level of participant satisfaction. However, they could not conclude efficacy for suicide prevention because the baseline rate for suicide was low. While use of counseling services could be considered a secondary measure of decreased suicide risk, the authors recognized the need for further studies with a larger sample size to measure reduction in suicidality or suicide rate.

One factor contributing to a steady increase in utilization of RFWP services is outspoken faculty endorsement. At grand rounds and other prominent forums, faculty leaders have provided consistently positive messaging regarding this program's importance as a means of promoting well-being in their own lives and having the potential to benefit all trainees.

Positive Feedback for a Multi-Faceted Wellness Curriculum

A wellness curriculum was included as part of a required leadership rotation within the Worcester Family Medicine Residency. The programming was a one-month set of workshops with homework assignments that sought to reduce the risk of burnout and indices of stress, among other objectives. Each session included an informational, evidenced-based introduction to a central topic important to wellness, and imparted residents with practical, take-home skills. Topics included[15]:

- the science of burnout syndrome, recognition of signs and symptoms, and validated screening methods
- mindfulness exercises including breathwork and meditation
- narrative medicine and other reflection/sharing skills
- problem solving to reduce barriers toward attaining work-life balance and enhanced self-care

At the conclusion of the month of workshops, feedback was generally positive. At three-month follow-up, residency wellness scores showed an increase compared to baseline.

Although the Worcester program is not a model for all wellness curricula, it does embody success factors common to other programs nationwide, such as a dedicated and protected time commitment and a combination of didactics with practical skill-building.

A Team-Building Retreat Combats Burnout

Recreational activities have become integral to a culture of well-being in post-graduate training because they can help reduce stress. These events are often fun, well attended, and reflect the interests and needs of each residency program.

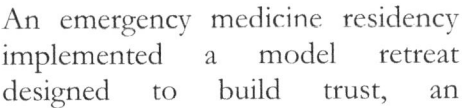

An emergency medicine residency implemented a model retreat designed to build trust, an organizational asset that enhances patient care while reducing the risk of burnout and depression. 25 residents participated. The post-event survey revealed a strong consensus that the activities were highly satisfying and that the event imparted a sense of group cohesion and collective accomplishment.[73]

Given the high level of participation and satisfaction with the retreat, the authors concluded that this low-cost activity could become an easily implemented intervention among other programs that wish to promote both well-being and resilience.

Mentorship Enhances Well-Being Among Surgical Residents

During post-graduate training, a formal mentor becomes more than a teacher. The mentor becomes a role model who continues to work with the resident to foster professional development.

Well before entering practice, there is a high prevalence of stress, job dissatisfaction, and burnout among otolaryngology-head and neck surgery residents (OHNSRs). A study presented evidence that a formal mentorship program (FMP) can improve well-being and reduce the risk of burnout among OHNSRs.[74]

Compared to baseline, the risk for burnout among FMP participants was reduced. The statistically significant burnout risk-reduction was evidenced by the Maslach Burnout Inventory in terms of all domains: emotional exhaustion, depersonalization, and reduced personal accomplishment. Stress level, as measured by the Perceived Stress Score, was reduced from baseline and at three-month intervals up to one year following enrollment. World Health Organization well-being parameters, including physical and psychological health, improved.

The study may have had confounding variables, but its results are consistent with other programs measuring positive outcomes of FMP on trainees. These data strengthen existing evidence that a formal, trainee-needs matched mentorship could provide lasting benefit in terms of burnout risk reduction and other efficacy measures shared by other wellness interventions.

Resilience Skill-Building Based on a Model to Help Military Families

A successful program that teaches resilience skills to military families who are coping with a loved one suffering from posttraumatic stress was adapted to pediatric residents who are challenged with patient-related grief. The study sought to use psycho-education to improve beliefs and self-efficacy among trainees who care for critically ill children. Investigators anticipated that a curriculum covering techniques for improving emotional regulation and trauma trigger management would be well received, while empowering residents to manage adversity.

Before beginning the first module, participating residents completed a pre-training survey that revealed a high baseline burnout risk, especially in the domains of emotional exhaustion and depersonalization. Participants then began a program consisting of six sessions covering wellness dimensions and resilience factors including [22]:

- emotional regulation/reappraisal
- problem-solving and goal setting
- communication with angry patients

After the final session, over three-quarters of participants reported that they were satisfied with the training. Surveys also indicated a high level of new insight and mastery of resilience interventions in the face of patient loss.

The authors seek to implement this curriculum in other residency programs to better assess trauma-informed resilience training as a means of reducing the risk of burnout in post-graduate medical education.

Well-Being Assessment Tools

One of the most important components of any wellness initiative is developing specific metrics to establish a well-being baseline and to follow a resident's or student's progress over time. Mayo Clinic developed a nine-question online well-being index that takes less than one minute to complete. It offers this validated assessment tool as a routine institutional performance metric to all its employees so they can compare their well-being against local and national standards. Mayo Clinic then guides and encourages its employees to use targeted resources to promote wellness.[75]

The Mayo Clinic's physician well-being initiative began in 2007 and undergoes regular assessments and improvements. Its mission is to "promote physician well-being through research, education, and development of individual and organizational well-being initiatives that optimize physician satisfaction and performance."[75] Interesting components of the program include monitoring physician leadership scores with tailored coaching to those in need, cultivating community through physician engagement groups, and incorporating discussions of career fit into annual reviews.

Wellness Innovation Including One of the First Chief Wellness Officers

Stanford has been growing its wellness program since 2011, when it established a wellness committee and hosted a conference of national wellness experts. In 2012, Stanford launched its WellMD website (wellmd.stanford.edu) and opened a crisis hotline.[76] Over subsequent years Stanford funded a physician wellness center, offered mindfulness and compassion programs, conducted its first wellness survey in 2013 with a follow-up in 2016, and created the first Chief Wellness Officer position at an academic medical center. In addition, to help reduce the burden of excessive paperwork for physicians, it instituted a scribe program.

Through innovation and by the incremental, systematic rollout and testing of its wellness initiatives, Stanford has grown its program into one of the top wellness programs in healthcare.

"Wounded Healer" or "Second Victim" Program

In an effort "to mitigate sources of stress and burnout, and help clinicians develop personal and professional resilience," in 2016 Christiana Care Health System began the Center for Provider Well-being.[77] The Center incorporates a comprehensive wellness model in collaboration with other health systems.

One interesting component of the program is its work with healthcare providers who are involved in an unanticipated adverse patient event, medical error, and/or a patient-related injury. In many cases, this kind of event is a traumatic experience in which the clinician may feel responsible and that he/she failed the patient. Christiana Care has developed a caregiver team and outreach program specifically for these "wounded healers" or "second victims." It provides a confidential "safe zone" with peer support where physicians can express their thoughts and feelings. Services are available 24 hours a day.

A related service is the Writing as Healing Workshops. These promote reflective writing to relieve stress and improve physician-patient communication and empathy.

Wellness Wednesdays

Wellness Wednesdays, a wellness initiative developed by Johns Hopkins University, offers programs centered on well-being.[78] These events were created so that residents, clinical fellows, and physicians can drop in for 10-15 minutes when they have a break to get some healthy snacks, receive a massage, participate in outdoor yoga, relieve stress with pet-therapy dogs, get consultations on financial health, and visit with others. Wellness Wednesdays are held in the afternoon and early-evening hours to make it easier for people to attend.

This is just one component of the Johns Hopkins wellness initiative, which also includes physical, mental, and financial resources for well-being. In addition, the university offers educational resources regarding depression and suicide, and a full curriculum to foster resident resilience.

CHAPTER 18
THE RESIDENT'S ROLE IN CREATING A CULTURE OF WELLNESS

If your actions create a legacy that inspires others to dream more, learn more, do more and become more, then you are an excellent leader.

Dolly Parton

Core Areas of Physician Well-Being

Residency programs are required to implement wellness education. However, it takes more than an ACGME mandate to conceive, institute, and quality-check a wellness program that effectively reduces the risk of burnout, suicide, and depression while bolstering trainee resilience.

In many residency programs—from Florida to California and in obstetrics/gynecology, internal medicine, family practice, emergency medicine and other specialties—residents and fellows are taking an active role in establishing a culture of wellness. When asked to review or comment about their residency program's wellness interventions, residents generally provide positive feedback if they train in a culture of wellness that is[14,79]:

- responsive to unmet needs, conducting a needs assessment when conceiving of wellness interventions
- transparent, involving residents in faculty meetings and committees and encouraging active participation in program development and evaluation
- integrated into clinical didactics, making use of time in parallel with other learning opportunities

Customized, openly promoted wellness programs tend to implement and maintain a variety of interventions in three core areas that correspond to physician well-being:

Physical and Mental Health
- fitness and nutrition, including access to health clubs and easy access to healthy foods
- confidential counseling, resilience training, and screening for depression and suicidality

Social Support
- recreational activities and team-building events

Professional Development
- autonomy or a sense of control: mentoring practicing physicians for high-quality, positive feedback
- sense of competence: acknowledgement of accomplishments through direct observation as well as self-assessment for enhancing self-awareness of professional development

Your Program Wants YOU!

No one knows more about the stressors and challenges of medical training than the medical students, interns, residents, and fellows who persevere and cope with the daily realities of patient care. Perhaps you are aware of differences in coping levels. Maybe you and a colleague have had to calm, comfort, and offer words of support to a junior resident during a difficult on-call night. If you are like 50-75% of residents with symptoms of BOS, someday the person needing an emotional boost could be you.

Ten Action Steps for Wellness Leadership

There are several ways you can help lead the effort to build and maintain a culture of wellness where you learn and train[14,80]:

1. The first step is to practice what you have learned in this *CoreWellness* course. But don't stop there! Learn from other programs and from the literature to become a culture of wellness expert.

2. Find a mentor who can help you continually expand your wellness knowledge, skills, and influence.
3. Conduct a confidential survey among your colleagues to determine the kinds of interventions they would like to see as part of a well-being/resilience program.
4. Make sure your program screens for BOS and depression, and encourage participation among your colleagues to help establish baseline prevalence within your program.
5. Help develop and launch wellness interventions within your department, and provide evidence for effective interventions that need continued funding and support.
6. Be an advocate for the continued engagement of your colleagues. A few encouraging words, just a few minutes a day, can make a difference.
7. Participate in faculty meetings and committees dedicated to wellness programming and join your wellness committee, if possible.
8. Educate residents and medical students during orientation about the resources available to support well-being including social gatherings, workshops, and mentoring.
9. Attend local and national meetings where wellness initiatives are being discussed.
10. Conduct wellness intervention research. Present and publish your results.

Remaining a Wellness Advocate Amid Healthcare Culture Change

Physician wellness is crucial throughout your career and is a worthy goal that must not be taken for granted. From your work with attendings, faculty, and mentors you know that burnout risk is out there in practice. There is considerable variation in office efficiency, to the extent that some seasoned professionals are content while others are on the verge of burnout with very low work-life satisfaction. Even in a high functioning office setting with an established electronic health record (EHR) in support of value-based healthcare (VBHC), over 60% of clinical interactions may consist of a provider staring at a computer screen or tablet rather than directly engaging with the patient.[81] The gap between innovations designed to improve patient safety and satisfaction, and VBHC and the reality of delayed and/or problematic technology adoption, is part of the reality of healthcare.

As part of a complex interplay among forces seeking to improve patient satisfaction while reducing medical errors and containing costs, healthcare culture change seeks to benefit both patients and providers. The perception of positive outcomes and their formal measurement varies significantly depending on where you practice within an evolving landscape that consists of an alphabet-soup of delivery models, most notably the patient-centered medical home (PCMH) and accountable care organizations (ACOs). From the day you graduate residency, you will begin navigating office practice settings in the midst of acclimating to new systems, processes, reporting obligations, and technologies. Among stakeholders—from patients, to healthcare executives, to providers—there is a resistance to change that is probably evident to you today as you rotate in different settings.

You now know that advocating for your well-being is not selfish and that it should not be perceived as driven by self-interest. Instead, it is part of a movement to shepherd the change of healthcare culture for the better. Indeed, your wellness—and that of your colleagues—is woven into societal expectations for optimum health services and integrated into the realities of medical practice. Keeping doctors and healthcare providers fulfilled, both professionally and personally, means they must join forces to achieve what is known as the "Quadruple Aim" to improve[82,83]:
1. population health
2. the patient-care experience
3. cost efficiency
4. physician well-being

In support of this set of goals, your ongoing advocacy for physician wellness is essential. Further, such advocacy will be increasingly expected of you throughout your career.

A roadmap for advocating physician well-being during practice is not as simple as following GPS instructions. It will consist of some twists and turns—but these need not be hairpin, harrowing maneuvers! Instead, these should be steps you take deliberately, accepting some degree of uncertainty and understanding that trial and error may lie ahead in finding the setting most aligned with your values, goals, and needs. A few options on your continuing journey of well-being advocacy might include[14,82]:

- **Mentor a Student, Intern, or Resident**. Becoming a mentor allows you to nurture your original vision of what it means to be a doctor by imparting the values of humanism, empathy, and professionalism. Being in close touch with your original mission statement for the practice of medicine will help you see the larger picture: that the alphabet-soup of the healthcare culture evolution, from EHR to VBHC, represents facets of a process that supports patients.
- **Lead and/or Participate in the Change Process**. Your residency experience with leadership provides excellent credentials for the role of Chief Wellness Officer (CWO). If you are practicing in a large managed-care organization with a commitment to workforce wellness, as CWO you would have a vital say in representing colleagues on all matters of well-being, from improving office efficiency to supporting team-based collaboration.
- **Provide Burnout and Wellness Metrics**. Similar to the validated tools your medical school or residency program uses (such as the MBI or well-being indices), health organizations also rely upon metrics and data points to gauge the effectiveness of wellness interventions, not only at baseline but at key intervals throughout the year.

Once you have mastered the wellness/resilience skills attained during residency, you are well equipped to advocate for a culture of physician well-being. Putting your skillsets into practice will result in effective self-care that also enhances patient care. Commitment to advocating for a culture of wellness will become a win-win—not only for yourself, but for your patients, office staff, and organizational administrators as you continue to navigate a career toward maximum professional satisfaction.

CHAPTER 19
CREATING AN EFFECTIVE WELLNESS INITIATIVE FOR YOUR DEPARTMENT

The part can never be well unless the whole is well.

Plato

Introduction to Creating an Effective Wellness Initiative

Most departments, institutions, and medical schools have taken the first steps to develop a wellness initiative. Some are more comprehensive and advanced than others. Some are more effective than others. Some have created metrics to follow progress and outcomes. Many of these programs would welcome guidance in how to develop a program that has a greater likelihood for success.

This chapter describes a step-by-step approach to help you understand your department's specific needs, develop a pilot wellness program, get institutional support, and continuously iterate and improve. Although this chapter takes the perspective of developing a wellness initiative for a residency program, these steps and concepts can also be applied to the medical school environment.

Step 1: Understand the Scope of the Problem

There has been a growing awareness over the past several years that stress, depression, burnout, and suicide are significant issues for the healthcare community. They impact providers' quality of life, healthcare costs, and the ability to deliver high quality care, and they involve issues related to patient safety and outcomes.

Estimates of resident burnout are over 70% in some specialties and the physician suicide rate is double the rate for the general population. One staggering statistic is that there are approximately 400 physician suicides each year in the United States; this is equivalent to losing all the students in an entire medical school each year. To make that statistic more palpable, the authors will never forget the gut-wrenching feeling in May 2018 when a fourth-year medical student and a psychiatry resident, both from NYU, committed suicide within five days of one another.

A longitudinal research study by BMC Health Services reported that 28% of surveyed physicians had intended to leave the field within two years and that, after two years, 13% actually did leave. Furthermore, according to a 2017 physician burnout and turnover report out of Stanford, "physicians who are experiencing burnout are more than twice as likely to leave their organization within two years," and the cost of recruitment for each new physician is between $250,000 and $1,000,000 depending on the specialty.[84]

In 2017, the ACGME revised Section VI of its Common Program Requirements for all accredited residency and fellowship programs, regardless of specialty, to address well-being directly and comprehensively. The requirements emphasize that "psychological, emotional, and physical well-being are critical in the development of the competent, caring, and resilient physician."[13] As a result, it is no longer optional for residency programs to address wellness—it is now a mandate.

The ACGME's Clinical Learning Environment Review Program (CLER) released the CLER Pathways to Excellence Version 1.1 in 2017.[85] This integrates the focus area of duty hours, fatigue management, and mitigation into well-being, addressing four interrelated topics:
1. work-life balance
2. fatigue
3. burnout
4. support of those at risk of, or demonstrating, self-harm

These four interrelated topic areas provide the basic framework for a comprehensive wellness program developed to address the major drivers of burnout and depression within a department and/or organization.

Step 2: Conduct a Needs Assessment

It is vitally important to the success of any early-stage wellness initiative that you first evaluate the specific issues and needs impacting your department. One of the most important components in the fact-gathering phase is the development and deployment of a well-designed needs assessment survey.

Needs assessment is a process to determine the gaps between existing conditions and desired conditions, and this can often be accomplished by conducting a survey. The components of a needs assessment survey include the present state, the desired state, stakeholders, resources, barriers or constraints, metrics and evaluation, and measuring desired outcomes. A good survey instrument should be neutral and unbiased, meaning that it does not make assumptions on the part of the participant. It should also be brief enough to be completed within fifteen minutes, as this will increase the participation rate.

Needs assessments are only effective when you truly understand the desired state and the resources needed to reach your desired goals. You can then create the right program and process to best fit your department's needs.

Take a few minutes to complete the example survey below. This will help you assess the current state of wellness in your department, the current components of any wellness initiatives conducted within the department, existing gaps to fill in order to achieve optimal wellness in the department, new components that need to be developed, and priorities for future actions. It is important that all stakeholders participate in the needs assessment and planning process.

You should ask the following questions as you begin to define your department's wellness initiative. Please add to this list to help address any issues within your department that are not covered. The more information you gather during the needs assessment phase, the better your odds for success.

Present State	
What is the present state of your departmental wellness initiative?	
Are there any programs presently in place that can impact wellness within the department?	
What is the prevalence of burnout among your residents? (Use a validated metric to determine burnout and wellness levels.)	
What is the present level of burnout in the rest of your department, including faculty, students, administrators, and other healthcare providers with whom the department interacts?	
What validated metrics have you used to measure wellness? (If you don't have metrics yet, refer to Chapter 16, "Self-Assessment Tools.")	
Have other departments within your institution launched wellness initiatives? Can you learn from them?	

Desired State (Needs)	
What is the desired outcome of your wellness program? From your perspective what does "excellent departmental wellness" look like?	
What knowledge and skills do your staff and residents need to reach the desired state?	
What are the gaps in knowledge and skills?	
Stakeholders	
Who should be included in the program (what is the target group)?	
Who can influence the program?	
What tangential groups should know about the program?	

Resources	
What education and training resources are needed to achieve your wellness goals?	
Does the department have any wellness advocates or experts?	
What financial resources does the department have for this initiative?	

Barriers and Constraints	
What problems might impact the development of a wellness initiative?	
Are there clear expectations of the desired state of wellness?	
Do you have a culture in your department where stakeholders feel they are too busy to address wellness?	
Do stakeholders feel empowered to openly discuss their issues?	

Metrics and Evaluation	
How will you measure the desired outcome?	
How will you know if you have achieved the desired state?	
Financial and Leadership Support	
Have you calculated how much the wellness initiative will cost? Have you created a wellness budget within your department?	
What financial support is needed for your wellness initiative?	
Does the leadership support wellness initiatives within the institution? Can you count on financial support from the institution for your wellness initiative?	
Have you created a wellness ROI calculation to share with institutional leadership?	

Sustainability	
Do you provide ongoing feedback regarding the state of wellness to all of your stakeholders?	
Did you get institutional support for your wellness initiative?	
Other Areas You Want to Address	

Step 3: Establish a Department Wellness Committee

The purpose of a wellness committee is to provide the guidance, resources, and support needed to create a culture of wellness within the department. It can serve as a sounding board for testing concepts and ideas as well as for promoting and monitoring the program.

If it has the right representation, a wellness committee is invaluable. A committee should represent the diversity of the organization and can include:
- residency program director
- faculty and staff physicians
- residents
- medical students
- senior human resources representative
- psychologist
- social worker
- department chair
- representative from the GME office
- other interested parties, with the approval of two-thirds of the committee

Whenever possible the committee should be made up of people who are willing to volunteer rather than assigned participants. In all likelihood, volunteers will be more committed to the project.

The committee's duties and responsibilities can include, but are not limited to:
- gaining an understanding of the predominant drivers of issues such as stress, fatigue, depression, cynicism, and depersonalization
- surveying residents and physicians on an ongoing basis for burnout, depression, resilience, wellness, and work-life balance with validated assessment tools to understand the to state of wellness within the department
- researching internal wellness policies and practices
- researching best-in-class wellness initiatives at other organizations
- creating a wellness roadmap for the department
- monitoring pilot program results over a pre-established period of time (but no longer than a year)

- soliciting feedback from participants at the end of pilots, analyzing results, and making modifications as needed
- orienting new residents to the wellness program
- developing departmental wellness champions
- holding focus group discussions with various stakeholder groups
- developing a system for open lines of communications and a "safe" forum for resident and attending interactions
- assuring access to any needed services for burnout, depression, and suicidal ideation and eliminating the stigma for utilizing such services
- creating peer support and an advocacy network, and providing wellness coaching to foster a culture of wellness
- sharing successes and failures with other departments and the institutional leadership
- promoting the program to enhance visibility, developing consistent messaging and branding

Step 4: Review National Best Practices in Wellness From Leading Healthcare Institutions

Although researching best-in-class wellness initiatives at other organizations was described as a function of the wellness committee in Step 3, it will be expanded upon in this section because it is a crucial step. A dozen high-quality wellness models that have been implemented and published across the country were presented in Chapter 17, "Wellness Program Examples." Some of these wellness programs are aimed at reducing the sense of isolation and frustration experienced by many residents. Others attempt to increase collaboration and teamwork or improve resilience, while still others seek to improve work-life balance. The best programs incorporate all of these important elements.

Although there are no established wellness program standards, commonalities amongst many of these high-quality wellness models can serve as a possible starting point or blueprint for the development of your own program's wellness initiative. Some of these common elements include:

- **Assessment/Survey:** Resident well-being should be measured at regular intervals and is becoming a routine institutional performance metric used within many healthcare systems.
- **Wellness Committee**: Most departments are now forming a wellness committee, and many are also forming overarching wellness committees at the institutional level.
- **Resources to Promote Self-Care and Healthy Living**: Resources that focus on reflection and self-growth, mindfulness, healthy eating, and exercise and fitness are provided.
- **Resilience Building:** Most top wellness programs include resilience building. Residents must have the tools and capabilities to cope with stressors and bounce back from major adversities. Some programs are using the *CoreWellness Online* resilience skill-building exercises for this purpose.
- **Community Building:** In most top wellness programs there are ample opportunities for social/professional gatherings and retreats, including opportunities for residents to participate in community service. Events are often fun, are usually well attended, and reflect the interests and needs of the residents in the department.
- **Peer Support Programs:** Peer outreach programs are available to discuss how to deal with traumatic experiences, adverse events, and other general resident experiences.
- **Mentoring and Coaching:** With the inclusion of wellness metrics, areas of resident improvement can be identified. Many top programs are providing personalized mentoring and coaching to address areas needing improvement.
- **Work-Life Balance:** Most top wellness programs stress the importance of work-life balance. They evoke not only a sense of duty toward patients and professional excellence, but also encourage fun and relaxation with colleagues, family, and friends.
- **Branding the Initiative and Wellness Awareness Promotion:** Most effective wellness programs include internal (and some external) branding to create consistency

in messaging within the department and institution. They also promote the program by disseminating success stories.
- **Paperwork Reduction:** Some programs are starting to introduce scribes to reduce the administrative burden of physicians.
- **Career Discussion in Annual Review:** A few programs discuss career goals and directions on an annual basis with their residents. They also provide leadership programs to help residents advance their careers.
- **Chief Wellness Officer:** Some health systems are beginning to hire chief wellness officers to lead institutional, system-wide wellness initiatives.

Step 5: Design a Wellness Program to Meet the Needs of Your Program

There is no single "correct" solution for a wellness program to combat stress, burnout, and depression. The best wellness program for your organization is one that fits your institution's culture and addresses the common observable needs you identified in Step 2, the departmental needs assessment.

Seek Stakeholder Input

The more input into the design of your wellness program the better. Input from your wellness committee can help determine which issues should be addressed as the top priorities.

Try to include skeptics in the design process. Their points of view will often enhance the final approach by challenging you to test and modify your assumptions.

Include Standardized and Personalized Programs

It is best to have a mix of standardized and personalized programs within your wellness curriculum.

A standardized program such as *CoreWellness Online* is consistent across all residents, can assess residents' progress using objective measures, is mapped to wellness milestones, and has a focus on resilience skill-building activities that are valuable to all residents.

Personalize your program by first filling the gaps identified during your department needs assessment. This can be done by seeking out and modifying best practices from other programs around the country or by locally designing a program utilizing your wellness committee, faculty, and/or residents.

Start Small

Remember to start small so you have better quality control over the initiative. Craft your program so that it addresses the most common concerns and those that were determined to be priorities. Then add elements to the program over time to address as many of the eight dimensions of wellness as possible:
1. emotions
2. environment
3. finance
4. intellect
5. occupation
6. physical
7. social
8. spiritual (beliefs)

Set Goals and Plan to Measure Success

As the next part of the design phase, establish the current baseline for what you plan to measure in your program, and then set specific goals for what you would consider a successful program. For example, a goal might be something like, "The department will reduce its physician burnout measures by 25% during the first year," or "Patient satisfaction and safety will increase by 10%." These objective measures can provide you with a quantifiable number for a return on investment (ROI) report (see Step 8).

Based on the results of the program, you can determine if gaps still exist and maintain a continuous quality improvement process.

Step 6: Find a "Wellness Champion" to Support the Initiative

A wellness champion is a valuable resource in gaining support for your wellness strategy. Your wellness champion should be a member of the department who expresses an interest in wellness and demonstrates a willingness to help others. In addition, the champion must be able to dedicate time and effort to the project. It could be a faculty member or it could be a resident who has been nurtured through the leadership process described in Chapter 18, "The Resident's Role in Creating a Culture of Wellness."

Traits and habits of a good wellness champion include:
- personal interest in health and wellness
- knowledge of the scope of the problem of stress, depression, burnout, and suicide in residency
- desire to help others
- respected within the workplace
- able and willing to dedicate the time needed to take a leadership role
- high energy and personable

The wellness champion should serve on the wellness committee to help set policy and advocate for the residents. He/she should be a liaison to help communicate departmental values and philosophies, and should work to get everyone within the department to embrace a culture of wellness.

Step 7: Develop a Budget for Your Departmental Wellness Initiative

Once your wellness committee and departmental leadership have determined what elements are needed for your wellness initiative, the next step is to create a formal budget to make sure you can meet your departmental goals. It is best to start with the "ideal" wellness program you desire to achieve and then modify it based on budget realities.

The following process outlines a helpful approach to budgeting for a wellness initiative:

1. Set your financial goals for the wellness initiative (i.e., do you want the initiative to be cost neutral, or do you want to demonstrate savings such as increased staff retention and fewer clinical errors?).
2. Look at historical departmental income including profit and loss over the last five years.
3. Determine the departmental budget for the next year. Break it down into monthly revenue/expenses and profit/loss projections.
4. Determine what the department can spend on a wellness initiative. Create a spreadsheet that breaks down spending into monthly amounts.
5. Determine elements of an "ideal" wellness initiative within your department. It could include resident recreational outings, nutritional food available in areas where residents congregate, memberships to athletic facilities, individual psychotherapy sessions, emotional/spiritual coaching and mentoring, financial counseling, subscriptions to standardized wellness programs like *CoreWellness Online*, professional/leadership development activities (such as sending residents or faculty to courses on wellness, society meetings for poster or live presentations, or the ACGME annual meeting), posting to websites and social media resources, etc.
6. Prioritize each element of the wellness initiative. Rank-order them from most important to least important.
7. Determine the projected cost of each element of the wellness initiative. Break it down into fixed costs such as salaries (if there are any related to the wellness initiative), subscription fees for standardized wellness programs, and healthcare facility memberships. Also account for variable expenses like recreational outings, food, and travel.
8. Determine if and how the elements of the wellness initiative should be phased in over the year. Are there specific months where there is a greater concentration of efforts (for

example, new residents getting a wellness orientation each year in July)?
9. Determine how much institutional support will be needed to cover the difference between the cost of the wellness initiative and the amount the department can spend on it. Review Step 8 to maximize your chances for getting leadership's financial support for your wellness initiative.
10. Track components of the wellness initiative with objective metrics. Also use some subjective measurements, such as departmental surveys regarding perception of the success of various components of the wellness initiative. This will help you improve or eliminate aspects of the program that are not working well and maximize financial efficiency.
11. Track financial results by looking at projected monthly costs versus actual costs (see the example table on the next page).
12. Adjust your wellness initiative as needed based on actual departmental income and expenses throughout the year. You will find that your projections become more accurate each year.

Description of Element of the Wellness Initiative (by Priority)	Rollout Date (Month & Year)	Fixed Cost or Variable Expense?	Projected Cost ($)	Actual Cost ($)	Modification Needed?
1.					
2.					
3.					
4.					
5.					
6.					
7.					
8.					
9.					
10.					
11.					
12.					
Total Costs:					

Step 8: Get Buy-In From Senior Level Management at Your Institution

Although there are obvious humanistic, moral, and ethical reasons for institutions to have comprehensive and successful wellness initiatives, there are also many competing budget priorities. The more you can create a business case to justify your departmental wellness initiative to institutional leadership with data demonstrating financial ROI, the more likely you will be to get the needed financial support.

Determine the institutional (or departmental) economic costs of burnout related to staff turnover, lowered quality of patient care, and decreased patient satisfaction scores. Turnover leads to recruitment costs, lost revenue during recruitment, lower department productivity, and expenses associated with onboarding.[86,87] The average cost to replace a physician is $500,000-$1,000,000.[88,89] A small change in productivity, even 1-2%, can have a large impact on an institution's bottom line.

Staff Turnover:
- decreased productivity[90]
- decreased revenue from seeing fewer patients
- decreased revenue to the institution related to fewer admissions, fewer surgeries, less imaging, and fewer grants[91]

Lower Quality of Patient Care:
- more medical errors and litigation[92]
- failure to discuss treatment options
- failure to fully answer patient questions
- less effective teamwork
- longer post-discharge recovery time

Decreased Patient Satisfaction:
- physician satisfaction is directly linked to patient satisfaction.[93]
- decreased patient adherence to physician recommendations[94]

Let's do a quick financial calculation for physician turnover, which is only one of the many financial impacts of burnout. If you can reduce the turnover rate related to burnout in an institution of 500 physicians from 5% to 2.5% annually, you will save the institution $6,250,000 per year (assuming a physician replacement cost of $500,000):

25 lost physicians X $500,000 = $12,500,000 at 5% turnover
12.5 lost physicians X $500,000 = $6,250,000 at 2.5% turnover
$12,500,000 - $6,250,000 = $6,250,000 savings annually

An institution may be willing to put 10-20% of these savings into wellness initiatives to reduce the physician burnout rate for the institution.

Remember that the above calculation does not include the loss of revenue related to fewer admissions, fewer surgeries, less imaging, fewer grants, an increase in medical errors and malpractice litigation, and turnover of staff members other than physicians. Institutional leadership will see the value of your wellness-initiative ROI.

A word of caution: there are instances of programs not being funded when claims of ROI were perceived as being too great (and therefore not believable by institutional leadership). An example of this was a work-life services program within an institution that consistently claimed a 7:1 ROI. It was terminated after a short time when institutional leadership dismissed their claims. Programs with a 2-3:1 ROI are believable and generally very acceptable. It is important to understand the financial goals of senior leadership regarding wellness programs. Keep in mind that senior management is often not looking at these programs as profit centers, but rather to be at least *cost neutral*.

Step 9: Start Small and Launch Pilots

Writer, futurist, and businessman Alvin Toffler once said, "You've got to think about big things while you're doing small things, so that all the small things go in the right direction." There is a lot of wisdom and insight packed into that quote that can be used as you strategically roll out your wellness initiative.

First, you must see the big picture and understand the desired endpoint for any new initiative. Then you must break down the big initiative into smaller component parts. Start small and launch the component parts carefully and thoughtfully with pilot testing. Begin with low-resource, high-impact initiatives that will go a long way towards increasing resident wellness. Don't initiate too many components at once or you won't be able to determine what is working well and what is not.

Create metrics so you will be able to measure success. Act on findings and make adjustments along the way so that each component part is moving in the right direction. This will help you reach your goals and realize the big picture.

If certain strategies are being underutilized or are falling short of expectations, you may want to do some internal marketing before eliminating a program. It may be worthwhile to feature success stories, provide protected time, or even offer participation awards as a means of garnering early acceptance for your program.

At the end of the pilot period, present senior management with detailed results of the wellness initiative broken down to its various components. Effective and ongoing communication is one of the keys to success for institutional support.

Step 10: Create Metrics to Track Results

In Chapter 16, "Self-Assessment Tools," 26 questionnaires and descriptions of what they measure were provided and broken down into five categories:

1. happiness and wellness
2. resilience and optimism
3. burnout and depression
4. character strengths
5. meaning in life and work-life balance

Review these questionnaires and determine which would be most useful for your department. Measure pre-, intra-, and post-intervention levels of wellness, burnout, depression, resilience, and meaning in life to determine the impact of your wellness initiatives. You can measure these at regular intervals and act on findings to make appropriate adjustments along the way, ensuring that each program component is moving in the right direction.

Then add other useful and important metrics such as:
- determining the amount of improvement of residents' knowledge and understanding regarding wellness
- assessing stakeholders' perceptions of the wellness initiative
- assessing the timely achievement of your department's goals along its wellness roadmap
- evaluating the effectiveness of wellness champions within the department
- monitoring access to services for burnout, depression, and suicidal ideation while eliminating any associated stigma
- determining the efficacy of wellness coaching
- fine tuning expense assumptions and projections
- accurately calculating ongoing ROI

Keep in mind that residency program philosophies, departmental and institutional leadership, and mandates regarding wellness competencies/milestones can change over time. It is critical for the long-term success of any wellness initiative to have ongoing evaluations (at least yearly) with improvement processes in place. The wellness committee should oversee the quality assessment and improvement process.

Step 11: Publish Your Process and Results to Become a "Wellness Influencer"

Throughout this book, you have read about some of the most successful wellness ideas and initiatives developed by residency programs and institutions across the United States. You have been provided with a step-by-step approach to create, assess, and improve your own wellness initiative.

After you have fully developed your program, assessed its effectiveness, and evaluated its ROI, share this information with other departments within your institution and health system. Also share your successes and setbacks through posters, local and national presentations, and peer-reviewed publications to establish your program as a national role model and become a "Wellness Influencer."

Step 12: Provide Feedback to the Authors

As the authors of this book, we hope you have found value in the information provided. We welcome your comments, thoughts, and insights. Please feel free to communicate with us at wellness@casenetwork.com regarding your path to achieving a culture of wellness.

CHAPTER 20
QUIZ

There are no secrets to success. It is the result of preparation, hard work, and learning from failure.

General Colin Powell

Please complete this series of questions to test your knowledge and determine your grasp of the materials presented in this book. Choose the single best answer for each question. After answering all 20 questions, review the explanations provided at the end of this chapter.

Questions

1. Which of the following statements most accurately characterizes the onset or prevalence of burnout syndrome (BOS) among physicians and doctors-in-training?
    A. It is highest among first year medical students.
    B. Symptoms most likely begin upon entering practice
    C. The prevalence is over 50% across several specialties.
    D. The prevalence is under 25% among allergists.

2. What is the percentage of doctors with BOS who also express suicidal ideation?
    A. 6%
    B. 12%
    C. 24%
    D. 48%

3. Three months into internship, a PGY-1 tells her roommate that she feels like a "supercharged robot: smart, fast, but numb to it all." Colleagues notice that she is becoming increasingly rushed, frustrated, less patient, and occasionally curt or rude to patients. One day she confided in her senior resident, an MD-PhD, stating sarcastically that she can't believe the attendings all think she is "so efficient," referring to her favorable evaluations. She added, "What's the point? Don't they see patients could care less? No matter how hard I try, no one listens to me? I wish I could go into research like you." Which of the following terms best describes this intern's psychological response to training stressors?
    A. Depersonalization
    B. Depressed mood
    C. Lack of personal accomplishment
    D. Suicidality

4. Which of the following personality traits increases the risk of BOS?
    A. Laziness
    B. Neuroticism
    C. Optimism
    D. Passion

5. Which of the following best describes how residents and medical students can implement or improve wellness programming?
    A. Meet with a mentor regularly
    B. Participate in wellness workshops
    C. Promote twice-yearly burnout screening
    D. Take part in outings

6. A second-year resident did her best to stabilize a patient admitted in critical condition, but the patient died within hours after admission. The PGY-2 had a busy night ahead and continued to admit patients. The following morning, she struggled to hold back tears when filling out her patient's death certificate. Which of the following options describes a possible sequalae that best fits this scenario?
    A. Enhanced competence
    B. Higher PHEEM score
    C. Higher sense of autonomy
    D. Second victim syndrome

7. Which of the following are NOT resilience traits or resilience-building practices?
    A. Jogging 30 minutes each day
    B. Reframing negative thoughts
    C. Sharing patient care experiences
    D. Trusting in personal coping ability

8. Which statement best explains why it is important to screen for depression in someone with a likely diagnosis of BOS?
    A. Depression screening has a higher yield among medical students with burnout than among residents.
    B. Most with BOS suffer from psychosis.
    C. Suicidal thoughts are not likely in those with BOS.
    D. There is substantial overlap between BOS and depression.

9. Which mental-health screening tool is mismatched with the measure or psychological state it is designed to identify?
    A. Maslach Burnout Inventory (MBI) – Emotional regulation
    B. PHQ-2 – Suicide risk
    C. Postgraduate Hospital Education Environment Measure (PHEEM) – Well-being among residents
    D. WHO-5 – Well-being

10. What intervention would likely benefit an intern who scored 50 on a CD-25 confidential survey?
    A. A sleep study
    B. An anti-depressant
    C. Regular exercise
    D. Resilience skill-building

11. Which statement best characterizes how faculty mentorship can enhance resident wellness?
    A. Community mentors are of highest quality when nearing retirement.
    B. Residents find formal mentors who are distinguished faculty members intimidating and could increase burnout risk compared to community-based mentors.
    C. The resident-mentor relationship has the potential to bolster trainee autonomy.
    D. Well published faculty members are the best success role models.

12. Your residency program/medical school is considering implementing a comprehensive wellness initiative. Which of the following options describes the best method for introducing the program?
    A. Combine wellness screens
    B. Try out one aspect of the program first
    C. Use post-event opinion survey data
    D. Write a needs assessment

13. Why would the WHO-5 wellness survey NOT be the best sole indicator of resident well-being?
   A. A state of calm is not an applicable wellness dimension in post-graduate trainees.
   B. Positive mood is not assessed.
   C. Quality of sleep is not assessed.
   D. The questions do not capture a sense of autonomy.

14. After a resident delivers news of a patient's death, the family unexpectedly reacts in an accusatory manner. The resident did her best to care for this patient and is intellectually aware that the deceased family's anger is a manifestation of grieving. She is nonetheless very troubled by this experience. How could narrative medicine help this resident cope?
   A. Entertain her with good literature.
   B. Improve her public speaking skills.
   C. Make available more time off from her regular schedule.
   D. Provide insight from colleagues who have had similar experiences.

15. Which of the following options best describes resilience-building behavior?
   A. Exercise regularly.
   B. Keep a thought journal to improve self-awareness of dysfunctional beliefs.
   C. Sleep.
   D. Try new forms of recreation.

16. Which of the following is a dimension of wellness outlined by the U.S. Department of Health and Human Services?
   A. Emotional
   B. Environmental
   C. Financial
   D. Occupational
   E. All of the above

17. Which of the following is a correct match between the consequence and its corresponding belief?
    A. **Consequence:** Anger. **Belief:** You are negatively comparing yourself to others.
    B. **Consequence:** Anxiety or fearfulness. **Belief:** You sense a loss of self-worth or that there is a real-word loss.
    C. **Consequence:** Embarrassment. **Belief:** You think you have violated someone else's rights
    D. **Consequence:** Guilt: **Belief:** You perceive some type of threat in the future.
    E. **Consequence:** Sadness or depression. **Belief:** You perceive that your rights have been violated in some way.

18. All of the following are examples of thinking traps EXCEPT:
    A. Catastrophizing
    B. Mind reading
    C. Overgeneralizing
    D. Procrastinating
    E. Tunnel vision

19. All of the following are steps for putting things in perspective EXCEPT:
    A. Anchoring with a best case scenario
    B. Creating a Gaussian distribution curve
    C. Getting a group consensus on normal practices
    D. Imagining likely outcomes and solutions
    E. Thought deconstruction

20. All of the following are components of conducting a needs assessment EXCEPT:
    A. Design a program to meet desired needs
    B. Determine barriers and constraints
    C. Determine desired state
    D. Document present state
    E. Identify stakeholders

Answers

1. The correct answer is D. Both during post-graduate training and out in practice, burnout prevalence exceeds 50% with the highest rates reported among emergency medicine, ob/gyn, internal medicine, and family practice physicians. Among allergists/immunologists, internists and family doctors, the rate of BOS is over 40% and less than 50%. Symptom onset can occur any time: during medical school, in residency, or years after starting practice. However, there is a notable uptick in cases during the first few months of internship.[3]

2. The correct answer is B. Surveys of residents and practicing physicians reveal an approximately 12% prevalence of suicidal ideation.[4] The other statistics are incorrect with respect to thoughts of suicide, but it is important to note that doctors in training have double the rate of suicides compared to the general population.

3. The correct answer is A. Burnout syndrome results from prolonged exposure to a stressful working environment and is measured according to three dimensions or domains: emotional exhaustion, depersonalization, and reduced personal accomplishment. Among physicians and others in the health professionals, depersonalization is described as a cynical attitude toward one's patients or clients, manifesting as irritability and as a lost sense of idealism. Patients, preceptors, and colleagues could note such cynical behavior as lapses in professionalism. The PGY-1 described here exhibits primarily signs of depersonalization or cynicism, which is consistent with burnout syndrome. A low sense of personal accomplishment is not consistent with this scenario. One can be diagnosed with BOS based on high degree of emotional exhaustion and or depersonalization.[7] The scenario does not depict depressed mood or suicidal thoughts.

4. The correct answer is B. In addition to work-related stressors, certain personality types or traits increase the risk for burnout.[8] Neurosis is a personality factor characterized by reactive, labile emotional responses to stressful situations whereby an

individual is more likely to experience anxiety and feel self-conscious or vulnerable. The other options are not associated with BOS.

5. The correct answer is C. There are many ways residents can take a leadership role in creating a culture of wellness. In addition to surveying trainees to determine what colleagues need and want (conducting a needs assessment), interpreting the results of burnout and depression screening, both at baseline and following wellness implementation, are two essential steps. Good screening requires a high level of participation that is more likely to follow ongoing messaging that calls for participation in a confidential, information-gathering process.[14] The other choices describe well-being elements that a trainee can pursue individually.

6. The correct answer is D. Second victim syndrome (SVS) occurs when healthcare providers at any career stage experience feelings of guilt or self-blame after a patient in their care dies unexpectedly or following a negative clinical outcome. SVS could manifest as a sense of self-blame, severe anxiety, confusion, or depression.[22] Enhanced autonomy and competence are wellness measures associated with graduate medical training, assessed using the 40-question Postgraduate Hospital Education Environment Measure (PHEEM). Improved measures of wellness are not a good fit for this scenario, which describes a trainee struggling to come to terms with a patient's death.

7. The correct answer is A. Regular exercise, along with healthy eating habits, are components of physical well-being that are often promoted as part of a wellness culture that fosters self-care, but they do not constitute resilience traits or practices.[5] Monitoring one's thinking for negative content, also referred to as *reframing*, can help residents cope with stressful patient encounters or situations. Self-efficacy generally increases with experience, as practitioners gain insight and trust into their ability to cope with the inevitable loss that comes with patient care. Medical students and residents can learn how to augment a sense of optimism early in their careers when challenged with the death of a patient. Narrative reflection is also a resilience

behavior, practiced through journaling or by sharing experiences with peers.

8. The correct answer is D. BOS and depressive disorders share symptoms, including anhedonia and anxiety. The two diagnoses are believed to co-exist in as many as 9 out of 10 subjects, according to one study, and there are those that refute that BOS and depression are distinct entities.[12] Moreover, in post-graduate trainees the prevalence of depression increases once BOS is diagnosed, necessitating dual screening. Psychosis is not a common feature of BOS or part of the diagnostic criteria.

9. The correct answer is A. Emotional regulation is a resilience trait, while emotional exhaustion—a loss of energy, sense of idealism, and profound physical fatigue—characterizes one of the three domains of burnout syndrome.[7] The other options are correctly matched. The WHO-5 is a survey used to measure well-being among the general population. PHEEM is a well-being instrument validated among post-graduate trainees. The Patient Health Questionnaire (PHQ) 9 or shortened 2-question PHQ-2 are depression screens.

10. The correct answer is D. The Connor-Davidson resilience scale (CD-25) consists of 25 statements for self-assessing resilience among five traits: personal competence, tolerance of stress, acceptance of uncertainty, sense of control over life, and spiritual influences. A score of less than 60 corresponds to low resilience. Scores should be reassessed at intervals for determining efficacy of resilience skill-building interventions.[32] This intern would benefit from resilience skill-building. The other choices do not describe interventions or measures pertaining to resilience.

11. The correct answer is C. Faculty mentors provide positive feedback that can improve a student or resident's sense of autonomy and self-confidence and reduce burnout risk.[74] Whether a mentor is a distinguished clinical researcher or based in the community has no correlation with burnout risk. The mentor's career stage does not factor into the mentor-mentee relationship.

12. The correct answer is B. Gradual implementation of a comprehensive wellness program often begins with a simple initiative that is easily planned and introduced. Quick turnout of positive feedback would inform next steps.[95] The other options describe data-gathering methods that, while important tools to shape an overall program, do not represent roll-out strategies.

13. The correct answer is D. Autonomy is defined, in part, as a sense of freedom to chart one's own learning course. Autonomy is an essential element of residency wellness.[5] Therefore the WHO-5, while in use among residency programs, is not the optimal wellness instrument as it was developed for the general population and measured against those with mental illness. On the other hand, WHO-5 *is* validated as a generic wellness measure based on health dimensions captured with five questions that relate to mood, stress, and energy level/sleep quality.

14. The correct answer is D. Narrative medicine is a resilience-enhancing, facilitated set of workshops where residents can learn coping skills for developing emotional intelligence, self-compassion, and patient empathy following challenging clinical experiences. During such sessions, the resident described in this question could benefit from her colleagues' shared stories of coping with the reality of medicine's limitations and the human dimensions of the healer. Students and residents, like their patients, also feel grief, anger, and guilt. Written accounts may be read aloud, not in an effort toward improving oratory delivery, but to heal with the help of a supportive audience of colleagues.[35,46] Assigned reading could be an element of narrative medicine workshops to set the tone and steer discussion during protected time without changing the duty schedule or detracting from days off.

15. The correct answer is B. Keeping a thought journal or using some means of recording emotions can enhance self-awareness of how stressors are related to emotions and behaviors. Medical students and residents find resilience-building exercises (such as taking the emotional temperature or undertaking a more self-analytical approach, where thoughts and beliefs are revealed as unhelpful and unfounded) can then lead to new ways of

reacting to adversity, with the potential to improve coping and resilience.[15] The other choices describe wellness practices that are not directly related to resilience training.

16. The correct answer is E. According to the U.S. Department of Health and Human Services Substance Abuse and Mental Health Services Administration wellness includes eight dimensions[1]:
    - **Emotional**: coping effectively with life and creating satisfying relationships
    - **Environmental**: good health by occupying pleasant, stimulating environments that support well-being
    - **Financial**: satisfaction with current and future financial situations
    - **Intellectual**: recognizing creative abilities and finding ways to expand knowledge and skills
    - **Occupational**: personal satisfaction and enrichment from one's work
    - **Physical**: recognizing the need for physical activity, healthy foods, and sleep
    - **Social**: developing a sense of connection, belonging, and a support system
    - **Spiritual**: expanding a sense of purpose and meaning in life

17. The correct answer is C. There are some strong and consistent connections between your B's and C's, including:

C: Feelings or Emotions	B: Beliefs or Thoughts
Anger	You perceive that your rights have been violated in some way.
Sadness or depression	You sense a loss of self-worth or that there is a real-word loss.
Guilt	You think you have violated someone else's rights.
Anxiety or fearfulness	You perceive some type of threat in the future.
Embarrassment	You are negatively comparing yourself to others.

18. The correct answer is D. Procrastination is not a thinking trap. Automatic thoughts are situation-specific thinking traps that go under the radar of awareness, containing reflexive self-appraisals, assessments of the immediate stressor, and beliefs about the stressor/adversity's impact on your future. Thinking traps include:

- **Jumping to Conclusions:** Believing something when there is little or no evidence to support it.
- **Emotional Reasoning**: Making the assumption that, in the face of adversity, your emotions are always accurate indicators of the nature of the adversity.
- **Magnifying and Minimizing:** Exaggerating the importance of certain aspects of a situation and diminishing others.
- **Tunnel Vision:** Having blinders or being unaware of the most important information about a situation, and instead focusing on insignificant details.
- **Mind Reading:** Assuming that you know what another person is thinking, or expecting another person to know what you are thinking.
- **Overgeneralizing**: Making broad assumptions, usually about lack of worth of yourself or others, based on very specific evidence.
- **Personalizing:** The tendency to automatically attribute the cause of an adversity to one's personal characteristics or actions. This is the opposite of externalizing.
- **Externalizing:** The tendency to automatically attribute the cause of an adversity to another person or to circumstances. This is the opposite of personalizing.
- **"Musting" and "Shoulding"**: Overly inflexible ideas or expectations of others or of oneself.
- **All-or-Nothing Thinking:** Viewing situations on one extreme or another instead of on a continuum.
- **Catastrophizing:** Assuming the worse possible outcome rather than positive or neutral ones.
- **Disqualifying or Discounting the Positive:** Telling yourself that the good things that happen to you don't count.
- **Labeling**: Assessing someone's character generally, using an umbrella term, based on one instance of a behavior.

19. The correct answer is C. Catastrophizing happens when we imagine the worst possible outcome of an action or event. It is cognitive distortion that makes a situation into a catastrophe when it is not. There is a scientific approach to put things in perspective that includes:
    - Step 1: thought deconstruction
    - Step 2: anchoring with a best-case scenario
    - Step 3: creating a Gaussian distribution curve
    - Step 4: imagining likely outcomes and solutions

20. The correct answer is A. Needs assessment is a process to identify gaps between existing conditions and desired conditions and is an early step in designing a program. One method of assessing needs is by conducting a survey. The components of a needs assessment survey include:
    - the present state
    - the desired state
    - stakeholders
    - resources
    - barriers or constraints
    - metrics and evaluation
    - measuring desired outcomes

REFERENCES

1. The eight dimensions of wellness. Substance Abuse and Mental Health Services Administration, US Department of Health and Human Services website. https://www.samhsa.gov/wellness-initiative/eight-dimensions-wellness. Updated October 24, 2017. Accessed January 16, 2019.

2. Konopasek L, Bernstein C. Combating burnout, promoting physician well-being: building blocks for a healthy learning environment in GME. ACGME Summer Spotlight Webinar; July 13, 2016. https://www.acgme.org/Portals/0/PDFs/Webinars/July_13_Powerpoint.pdf

3. Ey S, Moffit M, Kinzie JM, Brunett PH. Feasibility of a comprehensive wellness and suicide prevention program: a decade of caring for physicians in training and practice. *J Grad Med Educ.* 2016 Dec; 8(5): 747–753. https://www.ncbi.nlm.nih.gov/pmc/articles/PMC5180531/

4. Raj KS. Well-being in residency: a systematic review. *J Grad Med Educ.* 2016 Dec; 8(5): 674–684. https://www.ncbi.nlm.nih.gov/pmc/articles/PMC5180521/

5. Gunderman R. The root of physician burnout. *The Atlantic.* Aug 27, 2012. https://www.theatlantic.com/health/archive/2012/08/the-root-of-physician-burnout/261590/. Accessed January 13, 2019.

6. Maslach C, Leiter MP. Understanding the burnout experience: recent research and its implications for psychiatry. *World Psychiatry* 2016; 15:103–111. https://www.ncbi.nlm.nih.gov/pmc/articles/PMC4911781/.

7. Iorga M, Socolov V, Muraru D, et al. Factors influencing burnout syndrome in obstetrics and gynecology physicians. *Biomed Res Int.* 2017:Vol. 2017, Article ID 9318534, 10 pages. https://doi.org/10.1155/2017/9318534.

8. Baker K, Sen S. Healing medicine's future: prioritizing physician trainee mental health. *AMA J Ethics.* 2016 Jun 1; 18(6): 604–613. https://www.ncbi.nlm.nih.gov/pmc/articles/PMC5503146/

9. Neal JM. Physician burnout: American College of Physicians (ACP). The ACP Wellness Champions Initiative. https://www.acponline.org/system/files/documents/about_acp/chapters/in/16mtg/neal_wellness_champion.pdf. Published 2015.

10. Shanafelt TD, Boone S, Tan L, et al. Burnout and satisfaction with work-life balance among US physicians relative to the general US population. *Arch Intern Med.* 2012;172(18):1377-1385.

11. Bianchi R, Schonfeld IS, Laurent E. Is it time to consider the "burnout syndrome" a distinct illness? *Front Public Health.* 2015; 3: 158. https://www.ncbi.nlm.nih.gov/pmc/articles/PMC4459038/

12. ACGME Common Program Requirements. Accreditation Council for Graduate Medical Education. http://www.acgme.org/Portals/0/PFAssets/ProgramRequirements/CPRs_2017-07-01.pdf. Updated February 2017.

13. Okanlawon T. Physician wellness: preventing resident and fellow burnout, STEPS in practice. https://www.stepsforward.org/modules/physician-wellness. Updated 2018. Accessed February 10, 2018.

14. Runyan C, Savageau JA, Potts S, Weinreb L. Impact of a family medicine resident wellness curriculum: a feasibility study. *Med Educ Online.* 2016 Jan;21(1). http://www.tandfonline.com/doi/full/10.3402/meo.v21.30648

15. World Health Organization (WHO). Mental health: a state of well-being. http://www.who.int/features/factfiles/mental_health/en/. Updated August 2014. Accessed February 2018.

16. Linton MJ, Dieppe P, Medina-Lara A. Review of 99 self-report measures for assessing well-being in adults: exploring dimensions of well-being and developments over time. *BMJ Open.* 2016 Jul 7;6(7): e01064. https://wwwhttps://www.ncbi.nlm.nih.gov/pmc/articles/PMC4947747/

17. Topp C, W, Østergaard S, D, Søndergaard S, Bech P. The WHO-5 well-being index: a systematic review of the literature. *Psychother Psychosom* 2015;84:167-176. https://www.karger.com/Article/FullText/376585#

18. Diener E. Understanding scores on the satisfaction with life scale. University of Illinois, Department of Psychology. http://internal.psychology.illinois.edu/~ediener/Documents/Understanding%20SWLS%20Scores.pdf. Published 2006. Accessed March 1, 2018.

19. Clapham M, Wall D, Batchelor A. Educational environment in intensive care medicine—use of Postgraduate Hospital Educational Environment Measure (PHEEM). *Med Teach.* 2007; 29(6).

20. Chmitorz A, Kunzler A, Helmreich I, et. al. Intervention studies to foster resilience – A systematic review and proposal for a resilience framework in future intervention studies. *Clin Psychol Rev.* 2017;59:78-100.

21. Bird A, Pincavage AT. Initial characterization of internal medicine resident resilience and association with stress and burnout. *J Biomed Educ.* 2016: vol. 2016, Article ID 3508638, 4 pages. https://doi.org/10.1155/2016/3508638.

22. Bursch B, Lloyd J, Mogil C, et. al. Adaptation and evaluation of military resilience skills training for pediatric residents. *J Med Educ Curric Dev.* 2017 Jan-Dec;4:2382120517741298. https://www.ncbi.nlm.nih.gov/pmc/articles/PMC5736280/.

23. Halverson JL. Cognitive behavioral therapy for depression—overview. Medscape. https://emedicine.medscape.com/article/2094696-overview#showall. Updated Feb 28, 2018. Accessed Mar 12, 2018.

24. Cully JA, Teten AL. *A therapist's guide to brief cognitive behavioral therapy.* Houston, TX: Department of Veterans Affairs South Central MIRECC; 2008. https://depts.washington.edu/dbpeds/therapists_guide_to_brief_cbtmanual.pdf

25. Iacoviello BM, Charney DS. Psychosocial facets of resilience: implications for preventing posttrauma psychopathology, treating trauma survivors, and enhancing community resilience. *Eur J Psychotraumatol.* 2014; 5: 10.3402/ejpt.v5.23970. https://www.ncbi.nlm.nih.gov/pmc/articles/PMC4185137/

26. Wu G, Feder A, Cohen H, et al. Understanding resilience. *Front Behav Neurosci.* 2013; 7: 10. https://www.ncbi.nlm.nih.gov/pmc/articles/PMC3573269/

27. Reivich K, Shatte A. *The Resilience Factor.* New York, NY: Broadway Books; 2002.

28. Otani K, Suzuki A, Matsumoto Y, Shirata T. Relationship of negative and positive core beliefs about the self with dysfunctional attitudes in three aspects of life. *Neuropsychiatr Dis Treat.* 2017; 13: 2585–2588. https://www.ncbi.nlm.nih.gov/pmc/articles/PMC5648313/

29. Yan Y, Wang J, Yu W, et al. Young schema questionnaire: factor structure and specificity in relation to anxiety in Chinese adolescents. *Psychiatry Investig* 2018;15(1):41-48. https://www.ncbi.nlm.nih.gov/pmc/articles/PMC5795029/pdf/pi-15-41.pdf

30. Childress MD. From doctors' stories to doctors' stories, and back again. *AMA J Ethics*. March 2017;19(3):272-280. doi:10.1001/journalofethics.2017.19.03.nlit1-1703.

31. Orellana-Rios CL, Radbruch L, Kern M, et al. Mindfulness and compassion-oriented practices at work reduce distress and enhance self-care of palliative care teams: a mixed-method evaluation of an "on the job" program. *BMC Palliat Care*. 2017;17(1):3. Published 2017 Jul 6. doi:10.1186/s12904-017-0219-7

32. Cosco TD, Kaushal A, Richards M, Kuh D, Stafford M. Resilience measurement in later life: a systematic review and psychometric analysis. *Health Qual Life Outcomes*. 2016;14:16. Published 2016 Jan 28. doi:10.1186/s12955-016-0418-6

33. Seligman MEP. *Authentic Happiness*. New York, NY: Free Press; 2002.

34. Villarreal SS, Nash W, Cole TR. Nurturing the healers: a unique program to support residents. *J Grad Med Educ*. 2016;8(4):498-499. https://www.ncbi.nlm.nih.gov/pmc/articles/PMC5060936/

35. Bird A, Pincavage AT. A curriculum to foster resident resilience. *MedEdPORTAL*. 2016;12:10439. https://doi.org/10.15766/mep_2374-8265.10439

36. Beach MC, Roter D, Korthuis PT, et al. Multicenter study of physician mindfulness and health care quality. *Ann Fam Med*. 2013 Sep; 11(5): 421–428. https://www.ncbi.nlm.nih.gov/pmc/articles/PMC3767710/

37. Managing stress and distress. National Comprehensive Cancer Network (NCCN) website. https://www.nccn.org/patients/resources/life_with_cancer/distress.aspx. Accessed January 13, 2019.

38. Epstein RM, Krasner MS. Physician resilience: what it means, why it matters, and how to promote it. *Acad Med*. 2013;88:301–303. doi: 10.1097/ACM.0b013e318280cff0

39. Mache S, Vitzthum K, Klapp BF, Groneberg DA. Evaluation of a multicomponent psychosocial skill training program for junior physicians in their first year at work: a pilot study. *Fam Med* 2015;47(9):693-8. http://www.stfm.org/FamilyMedicine/Vol47Issue9/Mache693

40. Peng L, Zhang J, Chen H, et al. Comparison among different versions of Connor-Davidson Resilience Scale (CD-RISC) in rehabilitation patients after unintentional injury. *J Psychiatry* 2014;17:6. https://www.omicsonline.org/open-access/comparison_among_different_versions_of_connor_davidson_resilience_scale_153.pdf

41. Beck A, Emery G, Greenberg R. *Anxiety Disorders and Phobias*. New York, NY: Basic Books; 1985.

42. Millings A, Carnelley KB. Core belief content examined in a large sample of patients using online cognitive behaviour therapy. *J Affect Disord*. 2015;186:275-283. http://www.jad-journal.com/article/S0165-0327(15)30302-5/fulltext#s0015

43. Siotis IP. CBT for depression. Strengthening Resilience; Training for Military Family Service Providers. https://www.cfmws.com/en/AboutUs/MFS/Tool%20Kits%20and%20Training/Documents/Cornwall%20Traning%202014%20Documents/CBT.pdf. Published February 2014.

44. Leahy RL. *Cognitive Therapy Techniques: A Practitioner's Guide*, 2nd ed. New York, NY: The Guilford Press; 2017.

45. Tversky A, Kahneman D. Judgment under uncertainty: heuristics and biases. *Science*, New Series 1994;185 (4157):1124-1131.

46. Winkel AF. Narrative medicine: a writing workshop curriculum for residents. *MedEdPORTAL*. 2016;12:10493. https://doi.org/10.15766/mep_2374-8265.10493.

47. Muneeb A, Jawaid H, Khalid N, Mian A. The Art of healing through narrative medicine in clinical practice: a reflection. *Perm J*. 2017;21:17-013. doi: 10.7812/TPP/17-013

48. Ofri D, ed. *The Best of the Bellevue Literary Review*. New York, NY: Bellevue Literary Press; 2008.

49. Arnold BL, Lloyd LS, von Gunten CF. Physicians' reflections on death and dying on completion of a palliative medicine fellowship. *J Pain Symptom Manage*. 2016;51(3):633-639. https://www.jpsmjournal.com/article/S0885-3924(15)00507-2/pdf

50. Ostriker A. *The Initiation*. https://poetrying.wordpress.com/2013/05/03/the-initiation-alicia-ostriker/. Accessed January 16, 2019.

51. Wheelock A. Nesting in a season of light. In: Ofri D, ed. *The Best of the Bellevue Literary Review*. New York, NY: Bellevue Literary Press; 2008:42-47.

52. Alexie S. War dances. *The New Yorker*. 2009, August 10. http://www.newyorker.com/magazine/2009/08/10/war-dances.

53. Huyler F. Power. In: *The Blood of Strangers: Stories From Emergency Medicine*. New York, NY: Henry Holt & Co; 2000:119-120.

54. Wolff T. Bullet in the brain. In: *The Night in Question: Stories*. New York, NY: Random House; 1996:200-206.

55. Merenstein JH, Wolfe S, Sauereisen S, et al. 55-word stories and care of the underserved. *Fam Med*. 2007;39(3):169-170.

56. Okwerekwu JA. How do young doctors find balance after a 28-hour workday? *STAT*. 2017. https://www.statnews.com/2017/02/06/doctors-work-life-balance/.

57. Pennisi LT. *She Makes the First Cut*. https://poetrying.wordpress.com/2013/05/07/she-makes-the-first-cut-linda-tomol-pennisi/. Accessed January 16, 2019.

58. Carey S. *The absolute worst thing*. Bellevue Literary Review: 2005. http://blr.med.nyu.edu/content/archive/2005/absoluteworst.

59. Shafer A. Making mistakes. In: *Sleep Talker: Poems by a Doctor/Mother*. Bloomington, IN: Xlibris; 2001.

60. Levy JS. *The Art of Medicine*. A reflective writing for a narrative medicine exercise. 2019.

61. Li STT, Frohna JG, Bostwick SB. Using your personal mission statement to INSPIRE and achieve success. *Acad Pediatr*. 2017;17:107–109. http://www.academicpedsjnl.net/article/S1876-2859(16)30500-9/fulltext. Accessed January 13, 2019.

62. Serwint JR, Bostwick S, Burke AE et al. The AAP resilience in the face of grief and loss curriculum. *Pediatrics*. 2016;138(5):e20160791. http://pediatrics.aappublications.org/content/138/5/e20160791. Accessed January 16, 2019.

63. Chew BH, Lee PY, Ismail IZ. Personal mission statement: an analysis of medical students' and general practitioners' reflections on personal beliefs, values and goals in life. *Malays Fam Physician*. 2014;9(2):26–33. https://www.ncbi.nlm.nih.gov/pmc/articles/PMC4399405/. Accessed January 13, 2019.

64. Tang Y, Changhao J, Tang R. How mind-body practice works—integration or separation? *Front Psychol.* 2017;8:866. https://www.ncbi.nlm.nih.gov/pmc/articles/PMC5445124/. Accessed January 13, 2019.

65. U.S. Department of Veteran Affairs (VA), Center for Integrated Healthcare. Progressive muscle relaxation (PMR) and body scan, Ver. 3.0. https://www.mirecc.va.gov/cih-visn2/Documents/Patient_Education_Handouts/Progressive_Muscle_Relaxation_2013.pdf. Published July 2013.

66. Chipidza F, Wallwork RS, Adams TN, Stern TA. Evaluation and treatment of the angry patient. *Prim Care Companion CNS Disord.* 2016;18(3):10.4088/PCC.16f01951. doi:10.4088/PCC.16f01951.

67. Peterson C, Seligman ME. *Character Strengths and Virtues: A Handbook and Classification.* New York, NY: Oxford University Press; 2004.

68. Salles A, Liebert CA, Esquivel M, Greco RS, Henry R, Mueller C. Perceived value of a program to promote surgical resident well-being. *J Surg Educ.* 2017;74(6): 921-927. https://doi.org/10.1016/j.jsurg.2017.04.006.

69. Lefebvre DC. Perspective: resident physician wellness, a new hope. *Acad Med.* 2012;87(5):598-602. doi: 10.1097/ACM.0b013e31824d47ff

70. Dotters-Katz SK, Chuang A, Weil A, Howell JO. Developing a pilot curriculum to foster humanism among graduate medical trainees. *J Educ Health Promot.* 2018;7:2. doi:10.4103/jehp.jehp_45_17.

71. Zaver F, Battaglioli N, Denq W, et al. Identifying gaps and launching resident wellness initiatives: the 2017 resident wellness consensus summit. *West J Emerg Med.* 2018;19(2):342-345. doi:10.5811/westjem.2017.11.36240.

72. Olson SM, Odo NU, Duran AM, Pereira AG, Mandel JH. Burnout and physical activity in Minnesota internal medicine resident physicians. *J Grad Med Educ.* 2014 Dec;6(4):669-74. doi: 10.4300/JGME-D-13-00396.

73. Cornelius A, Cornelius BG, Edens MA. Increasing resident wellness through a novel retreat curriculum. *Cureus.* 2017;9(7):e1524. doi:10.7759/cureus.1524.

74. Zhang H, Isaac A, Wright ED, Alrajhi Y, Seikaly H. Formal mentorship in a surgical residency training program: a prospective interventional study. *J Otolaryngol Head Neck Surg.* 2017;46:13. doi:10.1186/s40463-017-0186-2.

75. Program on physician well-being. Mayo Clinic website. https://www.mayo.edu/research/centers-programs/program-physician-well-being/mayos-approach-physician-well-being. Accessed January 6, 2019.

76. http://med.stanford.edu/news/all-news/2017/06/stanford-medicine-hires-chief-physician-wellness-officer.html. Accessed January 6, 2019.

77. Christiana Care Health System Center for Provider Wellbeing. https://christianacare.org/forhealthprofessionals/center-for-provider-wellbeing/. Accessed January 13, 2019.

78. Johns Hopkins University Health Services website. http://uhs.jhu.edu/wellness/. Accessed January 13, 2019.

79. Fortenberry KT, Van Hala S, Frost CJ. Establishing a culture of intentional wellness: lessons from a family medicine resident focus group. *PRiMER*. 2017;1:12. doi:10.22454/PRiMER.2017.597444

80. Eckleberry-Hunt J, Van Dyke A, Lick D, Tucciarone J. Changing the conversation from burnout to wellness: physician well-being in residency training programs. *J Grad Med Educ*. 2009 Dec; 1(2): 225–230. doi: 10.4300/JGME-D-09-00026.1

81. Heudebert GR. The Privilege of Being a Physician and the immutable values of the medical profession. *Trans Am Clin Climatol Assoc*. 2017;128:234-242. https://www.ncbi.nlm.nih.gov/pmc/articles/PMC5525415/

82. Sinsky C, Shanafelt T, Murphy ML, et al. Creating the organizational foundation for joy in medicine: organizational changes lead to physician satisfaction. AMA STEPS Forward; September 7, 2017. https://www.stepsforward.org/modules/joy-in-medicine. Accessed January 13, 2019.

83. Bodenheimer T, Sinsky C. From triple to quadruple aim: care of the patient requires care of the provider. *Ann Fam Med*. 2014;12(6):573-576. doi: 10.1370/afm.1713

84. Berg S. At Stanford, physician burnout costs at least $7.75 million a year. *AMA Online*. November 17, 2017. https://www.ama-assn.org/practice-management/physician-health/stanford-physician-burnout-costs-least-775-million-year. Accessed January 13, 2019.

85. ACGME. Clinical Learning Environment Review (CLER). CLER pathways to excellence: expectations for an optimal clinical learning environment to achieve safe and high quality patient care, Version 1.1. ACGME, 2017.

https://www.acgme.org/Portals/0/PDFs/CLER/CLER_Pathways_V1.1_Digital_Final.pdf Accessed January 13, 2019.

86. Landon BE, Reschovsky JD, Pham HH, Blumenthal D. Leaving medicine: the consequences of physician dissatisfaction. *Med Care.* 2006; 44(3):234-242.

87. Shanafelt TD, Sloan J, Satele D, Balch C. Why do surgeons consider leaving practice? *J Am Coll Surg.* 2011;212(3):421-422.

88. Schutte L. What you don't know can cost you: building a business case for recruitment and retention best practices. Association of Staff Physician Recruiters website. http://www.aspr.org/?696. Published 2012. Accessed January 2, 2019.

89. Noseworthy J, Madara J, Cosgrove D, et al. Physician burnout is a public health crisis: a message to our fellow health care CEOs. Health Affairs Blog. http://healthaffairs.org/blog/2017/03/28/physician-burnout-is-a-public-health-crisis-a-message-to-our-fellow-health-care-ceos/. Published March 28, 2017. Accessed January 2, 2019.

90. Shanafelt TD, Mungo M, Schmitgen J, et al. Longitudinal study evaluating the association between physician burnout and changes in professional work effort. *Mayo Clin Proc.* 2016;91(4):422-431.

91. Turner TB, Dilley SE, Smith HJ, et al. The impact of physician burnout on clinical and academic productivity of gynecologic oncologists: a decision analysis. *Gynecol Oncol.* 2017 Sep;146(3):642-646.

92. Hall LH, Johnson J, Watt I, Tsipa A, O'Connor DB. Healthcare staff wellbeing, burnout, and patient safety: a systematic review. *PLoS One.* 2016;11(7):e0159015.

93. Haas JS, Cook EF, Puopolo AL, Burstin HR, Cleary PD, Brennan TA. Is the professional satisfaction of general internists associated with patient satisfaction? *J Gen Intern Med.* 2000;15(2):122-128.

94. DiMatteo MR, Sherbourne CD, Hays RD, et al. Physicians' characteristics influence patients' adherence to medical treatment: results from the medical outcomes study. *Health Psychol.* 1993;12(2):93-102.

95. Parks T. AMA Wire. Redesigning the gas lounge: how residents changed their space. *AMA.* September 21, 2016. https://wire.ama-assn.org/education/redesigning-gas-lounge-how-residents-changed-their-space. Accessed January 13, 2019.

OTHER USEFUL RESOURCES

> **National Suicide Prevention Lifeline**
> If you are in crisis, call 9-1-1 or contact the National Suicide Prevention Lifeline at 1-800-273-TALK (8255) or https://suicidepreventionlifeline.org/

ACGME. Physician well-being, tools and resources. http://www.acgme.org/What-We-Do/Initiatives/Physician-Well-Being/Resources. Published 2013.

ACOG-CREOG. *Physician satisfaction and wellness initiative.* Physician wellness video. https://www.acog.org/About-ACOG/ACOG-Departments/CREOG/CREOG-Search/CREOG-Physician-Satisfaction-and-Wellness-Initiative. Published 2017.

Alliance for Academic Internal Medicine. Annotated bibliography of evidence based well-being interventions. http://www.im.org/p/cm/ld/fid=1683.

American Medical Association. Preventing burnout in medical residents and fellows: 6 keys for wellness. *AMA Wire.* https://wire.ama-assn.org/education/preventing-burnout-medical-residents-and-fellows-6-keys-wellness. Published January 20, 2016.

Association of Professors of Gynecology and Obstetrics. Teaching tips—role modeling. https://www.apgo.org/wp-content/uploads/2016/05/TT-Role-Modeling-1.pdf. Published 2016.

Bohman B, Dyrbye L, Sinsky CA, et al. Physician well-being: the reciprocity of practice efficiency, culture of wellness, and personal resilience. *NEJM Catalyst.* August 17, 2017. https://catalyst.nejm.org/physician-well-being-efficiency-wellness-resilience/

Busireddy KR, Miller JA, Ellison K, et al. Efficacy of interventions to reduce resident physician burnout: a systematic review. *J Grad Med Educ.* June 2017;9(3): 294-301. https://doi.org/10.4300/JGME-D-16-00372.1

Daskivich TJ, Jardine DA, Tseng J, et al. Promotion of wellness and mental health awareness among physicians in training: perspective of a national, multispecialty panel of residents and fellows. *J Grad Med Educ.* 2015;7(1):143-147. doi:10.4300/JGME-07-01-42.

Denq W, Zaver F, Liu L, Battaglioli N. Academic life in emergency medicine: jumpstart your wellness, inspiring residency initiatives. https://www.aliem.com/2017/01/wellness-inspiring-residency-initiatives/. Published January, 2017.

Eyre HA, Siddarth P, Acevedo B, et al. *Int Psychogeriatr.* 2017 Apr; 29(4): 557–567. https://www.ncbi.nlm.nih.gov/pmc/articles/PMC5540331/

Finkelstein C. Improving physician resiliency. *American Medical Association STEPS Forward.* https://www.stepsforward.org/modules/improving-physician-resilience Updated 2018. Accessed February 2018.

Hutter MM, Kellogg KC, Ferguson CM, Abbott WM, Warshaw AL. The impact of the 80-hour resident workweek on surgical residents and attending surgeons. *Ann Surg.* 2006;243(6):864-875. doi: 10.1097/01.sla.0000220042.48310.66

Joseph R. Performance training and public health for physician burnout. *NEJM Catalyst.* https://catalyst.nejm.org/performance-training-public-health-burnout/. Published March 15, 2017.

Lux KM, Hutcheson JB, Peden AR. Ending disruptive behavior: staff nurse recommendations to nurse educators. *Nurse Educ Pract.* 2014;14(1):37-42. https://doi.org/10.1016/j.nepr.2013.06.014

Minkove JF. The difference a wellness program can make. Johns Hopkins Medicine, News & Publications. https://www.hopkinsmedicine.org/news/articles/the-difference-a-wellness-program-can-make. Published October, 10, 2017.

Moss M, Good VS, Gozal D, Kleinpell R, Sessler CN. An official Critical Care Societies collaborative statement: burnout syndrome in critical care health care professionals: a call for action. *Am J Crit Care.* July 2016;25(4):368-376. doi: 10.4037/ajcc2016133

Murphy ML, de Vries P, Trockel M, et. al. Well MD Center, Stanford Medicine. Status Report. https://wellmd.stanford.edu/content/dam/sm/wellmd/documents/2017-wellmd-status-report-dist-1.pdf. Published March 2017.

National Academy of Medicine. Clinician resilience and well-being. https://nam.edu/initiatives/clinician-resilience-and-well-being/. Updated 2018. Accessed February 2018.

Osler Program's Resident Wellness Toolkit. Medicine Matters/Johns Hopkins Medicine website. https://medicine-matters.blogs.hopkinsmedicine.org/2018/03/osler-programs-resident-wellness-toolkit/. Published March 6, 2018.

Palamara K, Kauffman C. Stone VE, Bazari H, Donelan K. Promoting success: a professional development coaching program for interns in medicine. J Grad Med Educ. December 2015;7(4): 630-637. https://doi.org/10.4300/JGME-D-14-00791.1

Peckham C. Medscape national physician burnout & depression report 2018. Medscape: January 2018. https://www.medscape.com/slideshow/2018-lifestyle-burnout-depression-6009235

Purdie DN. Work-life balance: the true failure is in not trying. *Fronti Pediatr.* 2016;4:37. https://doi.org/10.3389/fped.2016.00037

SAMHSA. *The eight dimensions of wellness.* YouTube video. https://www.youtube.com/watch?v=tDzQdRvLAfM&feature=youtu. Published July 1, 2016.

Shaikh K. Resident wellness in graduate medical education (GME). NEJM Knowledge Plus website. https://knowledgeplus.nejm.org/blog/resident-wellness-in-graduate-medical-education-gme/. Published 2018.

Stringer H. Emotional survival skills for physicians in training: with the help of a psychologist, medical residents are learning how to cope with trauma and stress on the job. *Monitor on Psych.* 2017;48(2). http://www.apa.org/monitor/2017/02/emotional-skills.aspx

INDEX

A

A-B-C thought connections, 28
Accreditation Council for Graduate Medical Education (ACGME), 5, 17, 21, 162, 171, 184, 203, 204, 210, 213
ACE, 78, 80-87
Achievement, 14, 16, 33, 96, 97, 190
Alexithymia, 13
Anchoring, 92, 105, 107
Anger, 9, 32, 34, 53, 138, 139, 141, 142, 197, 201
Anxiety, 7, 17, 31, 102, 103, 207
Automatic thoughts, 32, 70

B

Behavior-ometer, 70
Breathwork, 9, 23, 41, 92, 132, 155
Burnout,
    patient consequences, 15
    personal consequences, 15
    prevalence, 15
    professional consequences, 15
burnout syndrome (BOS), 2-3, 5-6 12-17, 24, 36, 151, 163-164, 194-195, 198-200

C

Cognitive behavioral therapy (CBT), 27, 28, 38, 62, 80, 207
Cognitive distortion, 62
Cognitive restructuring, 80
Conflict management, 9
Connor-Davidson Resilience Scale, 35, 81, 145, 147, 200, 207
Core beliefs, 9, 33, 39, 70, 73, 78, 82, 93, 96, 99, 205
Crash cart resilience exercises, 9, 42, 140
Culture of wellness, 8, 10, 20, 21, 132, 150, 162-164, 167, 177, 179, 183, 191, 199, 213

D

Depersonalization, 13, 16, 194
Diaphragmatic breathing, 133
Dysfunctional thinking, 62, 70

E

Eight dimensions of wellness, 2, 182, 203, 215
Emotional exhaustion, 13, 16
Emotional temperature, 8, 40, 52-58, 62-66, 75, 76
Emotion-ometer, 69

G

Gaussian thought distribution, 9, 41, 102, 104, 107, 109

H

Humanism, 151

M

Managing conflict, 41, 139
Maslach Burnout Inventory (MBI), 16, 24, 196
Mind pulse, 8, 40, 44-47, 54, 56, 62
Mission statement, 9, 41, 123-130, 166, 208

N

Narrative medicine, 9, 41, 112-115, 122, 197, 201, 207-208
Narrative writing, 119
Neuroticism, 13, 195
Nucleus beliefs, 9, 33, 41, 96-99

P

Personal efficacy, 13
Positive Evidence Points (PEP), 9, 41, 77-82, 86-88
Postgraduate Hospital Education Environment Measure (PHEEM), 24, 195-200, 204
Progressive muscle relaxation (PMR), 134, 209

R

Reduced personal accomplishment, 16
resilience, 2, 4, 8, 10, 26, 27, 29, 31, 33-40, 44, 49, 53, 57, 63, 64, 67, 70, 75, 78-82, 86, 96, 99, 102, 112, 115, 117, 124, 126, 131, 132, 138, 139, 144, 145, 147, 151, 152-164, 167, 178-182, 190, 195, 197-201, 205-208, 213, 214, 220, 221
Resilience Factor Inventory, 36, 145

S

Satisfaction with Life Scale, 24, 145, 147
Seligman, Martin, 2, 206, 209

T

Tension-relaxation cycle (TRC), 134
Thought X-ray, 8, 40, 63-65, 70, 78
Thought balloons, 9, 93

Truth-ometer, 69

U

Unhelpful behaviors, 75

V

VIA Survey, 146-148
Visualization, 9, 41, 92, 132

W

Well-being, 2, 4, 5, 20-24, 44, 128, 144, 145, 150, 151, 154-167, 171, 180, 197, 199, 200, 203, 204, 209, 210, 213, 214
Wellness, i, ii, 2, 4, 8, 10, 18, 20, 22, 144, 150-155, 159, 160, 163-166, 177-183, 186, 190, 191, 203, 213, 214
Wellness initiative, 10, 136, 158, 160, 170-191, 196, 213
Wellness models, 10, 151, 179
WHO-5, 24, 144, 196, 197, 200, 201, 204
Worksheets, 46, 47, 58, 64, 65, 98, 109
World Health Organization (WHO), 4, 21, 204

Y

You-Dini, 8, 39, 40, 41, 79
You-Guru, 8, 39, 40, 63, 79

ABOUT THE AUTHORS

Jeffrey Levy, MD

Dr. Jeffrey Levy is a physician, author, entrepreneur, and an internationally recognized expert in e-learning. He is the Founder and CEO of CaseNetwork, a technology enhanced medical education and clinical decision support company. He is also a co-founder for the Institute for Surgical Excellence, a non-profit 501(c)(3) organization dedicated to improving surgical care and patient outcomes for emerging technologies. Prior to this, Dr. Levy was the Founder and CEO of Reflective Learning, where he developed online resilience and wellness education programs in collaboration with 20 of the top psychologists in the world. His online wellness programs had over 25 million hits and were featured in Time Magazine, O Magazine, Fitness Magazine, Ladies Home Journal, NBC, ABC, NPR, The London Times, USA Today, and more than 100 other newspapers across America.

For three decades Dr. Levy has been on the forefront of innovations in the medical field. Some of his accomplishments include developing one of the first virtual reality surgical simulators (the Virtual Reality Hysteroscope), creating some of the first interactive laser discs and CD-ROMs in medicine, producing some of the most sophisticated 3-D medical/surgical animations, and producing the first online case-based education in medicine.

He has worked with hundreds of subject matter experts, dozens of medical societies, and government regulators to advance medical/surgical education, training, and clinical practice. Through his award-winning programs, Dr. Levy has educated more than 400,000 physicians globally.

Dr. Levy has also served as the Medical Director of Education and Technology Initiatives for the University of Pennsylvania Health System, where his responsibilities included development of computerized physician and patient education systems. His other academic roles have included Associate Chairman of the Department of Obstetrics and Gynecology and Director of Resident Education and Medical Student Education at Albert Einstein Medical Center in Philadelphia.

Dr. Levy has been course director for over 70 courses, presented more than 200 national and international lectures, authored numerous abstracts and scientific papers, and developed several patents and inventions. He received his MD from the University of Missouri-Columbia Medical School and completed his residency in Obstetrics and Gynecology at Michael Reese Hospital and Medical Center in Chicago, Illinois. He had a clinical practice in Obstetrics and Gynecology for 14 years.

Dr. Levy's social mission is to provide high-quality education and training resources to increase the number of qualified healthcare providers throughout Africa. He is working with U.S.-based medical societies and clinicians in partnership with Ministries of Health and African clinicians to develop standardized, regionally relevant curricula for African healthcare providers.

Louis Neipris, MD

Dr. Louis Neipris is an accomplished medical writer with content expertise in wellness. His portfolio includes hundreds of print and online materials for health professionals and patients. Dr. Neipris has developed curricula based on principles of positive psychology and the stages of change model for adopting healthy behaviors. His work is featured on CaseNetwork and other user-customized, Web-based learning portals including interactive, evidenced-based modules focused on wellness/resilience, smoking cessation, stress reduction, and disease self-management.

Dr. Neipris obtained his MD from SUNY Health Science Center Brooklyn and has a BA in English from Columbia University. In addition to completing his pathology residency at the Mallory Institute—Boston Medical Center, he has clinical training at Mount Auburn Hospital of Harvard Medical School.

ABOUT CASENETWORK

CaseNetwork was founded in 2011 by a physician, Dr. Jeffrey Levy, with the vision to become the global standard for medical education by providing the most advanced and innovative learning framework across the continuum of education and training with the ultimate goal to improve patient care.

CaseNetwork is a technology-enhanced medical education company delivering competency-focused, case-based education that enables learners to improve their knowledge and comprehension of critical patient situations and disease states. CaseNetwork's simulated patient encounters integrate evidence-based clinical information with required proficiencies and skills. Its proprietary platforms include interactive decision-making and peer-to-peer problem solving that is conveniently delivered in a browser or on mobile devices for anytime, anywhere learning.

CaseNetwork is continuously innovating to provide the highest quality content coupled with the latest technological advances. It is committed to help healthcare providers around the world to learn faster, more efficiently and more conveniently. It strives to assist the next generation of healthcare providers become the most capable and competent possible in an ever-changing healthcare environment. For more information, visit www.casenetwork.com.

Made in the USA
Monee, IL
19 February 2020